Is Your Voice Telling on You?

How to Find and Use Your Natural Voice

Third Edition

Is Your Voice Telling on You?

How to Find and Use Your Natural Voice

Third Edition

Daniel R. Boone, PhD

PLURAL
PUBLISHING
INC.

5521 Ruffin Road
San Diego, CA 92123

e-mail: info@pluralpublishing.com
Website: http://www.pluralpublishing.com

Typeset in 11/13 Garamond by Flanagan's Publishing Services, Inc.
Printed in the United States of America by McNaughton & Gunn, Inc.

Library of Congress Cataloging-in-Publication Data

Boone, Daniel R.
  Is your voice telling on you? : how to find and use your natural voice / Daniel R. Boone, PhD.—Third edition.
       pages cm
  Includes bibliographical references and index.
  ISBN 978-1-59756-801-2 (alk. paper)—ISBN 1-59756-801-5 (alk. paper)
  1. Voice culture. I. Title.
  PN4162.B636 2016
  808.5—dc23
                                                    2015019520

Contents

Preface

Do you like your speaking voice? Does your voice serve you well (at home, at work, at play)? Does this book title, *Is Your Voice Telling on You?*, remind you that some of the time your speaking voice does not always represent the way you feel inside. The fact is, we don't always hear our selves as others do. And our voice is always changing in the various situations we find ourselves. Wherever we are or the situation we may be in, our voices should represent the real you.

When we first hear ourselves on some kind of voice playback, such as an answering machine, we ask the question, "Is that really me?" Hearing one's own voice on playback is often the first time we didn't like the way we sounded. Or we may over time be coming aware that our voices often "let us down." It may be only certain situations (like asking for a date, failing a job interview, or trouble making a sale) where our voices seemed to work against us.

Even when we realize that we have some kind of voice problem, most of us don't know what to do about it. *Is Your Voice Telling on You?* is a friendly way designed to help one find and use a better voice. With a little help, most of us can find and use a normal (or natural) voice, a voice that is distinctively our own, one that serves us well in the things that we do.

Over my long career as a speech pathologist, I have worked with people with voice problems in hospitals, university clinics, medical centers, and in private practice. I have worked as a vocal coach for athletes, actors, sales people, teachers, and politicians. I began to realize over time that most poor speaking voices were simply the result of people misusing their normal voice equipment: our lungs, vocal folds, and resonators. A good natural voice is a lasting voice produced with the right amount of effort, the right breathing, the appropriate pitch and loudness, with a balance of relaxation and tension.

Some kind of playback recorder (even a smartphone will do) will be essential as we listen and practice some of the voice exercises in the book. Former voice clients have told me they always did better practicing alone, such as in a bedroom or their office—many have found their car was a great place to practice working on voice. In this book we'll talk about some natural enemies that work against developing a better voice, such as how our emotions (fear, anger, happiness, etc.) shape the way our voices sound. Some of our emotions we can express in our voices, and some of them are better controlled, if not hidden. The environment, such as low humidity and dryness, directly influences the quality of our voices. Some voices are compromised by the medications we take. Tobacco or marijuana smoke can produce devastating change to the vocal folds and must be avoided by anyone wanting to have a better voice.

The self-tests and exercises in the book are easy to use. The good part of working on your own voice this way is that you should feel and hear some improvement in your voice almost immediately. It will take some time, however, before changes in voice become more automatic to use. A good voice, like a good appearance or personality, does not come with a cosmetic "quick fix," such as tucking in your stomach and standing taller, or showing a broad smile. For most of us, once the *natural* voice is found, it becomes an easier voice to use than the old voice we had before we found this book. Why? Because your *natural* voice is the *real* you.

—Daniel R. Boone, PhD
Tucson, Arizona

CHAPTER 1

Is Your Voice Telling on You?

"He looked like a leader—until he spoke."

We all have known people who never get out of their cars without combing their hair or checking their makeup. They may spend a lot of money on clothes, hair styling, cosmetics, and fitness. They may have had a fine education, taken classes on the Web, and read all of the books on how to win friends and influence people. Yet all of their efforts can be undone because they have never given much thought to how their voices sound.

Carl was one of those people. At age 32, he had a great resume to submit for a management job with one of our country's largest pharmaceutical houses. His favorable email correspondence and even his references set Carl up for his first in-person interview. When he opened his mouth to answer a few questions by his two interviewers, out came a slightly hoarse breathy voice, not quite loud enough to be easily heard. He did not get the position that he had trained for and wanted. Subsequent feedback told him that the interviewers thought he sounded fearful and too tense to handle a management position.

Although Carl required professional help by a speech pathologist to correct the more obvious problems in his voice, the most common voice problems are caused by people doing things that prevent them from having a natural or normal voice. We hear people continually using a poor voice but they have no idea on how to correct it: people like Samantha, 24, who lost her

1

job as a TV weather forecaster because of viewer complaints of her high-pitched, nasal voice; or Jamie, 29, whose voice sounded so effeminate that other men in the locker room joked about him behind his back; or the woman who was mistaken on the telephone for her husband, or the husband whose voice sounded like he could be his wife or his mother. What we sound like is what people think we are.

Unfortunately, although many people realize their voices do not represent them well, either generally or in certain situations, they don't know how to improve the sound of their voices. This is where this book can help you develop a better voice by finding your real natural voice. The natural normal voice is produced by an easy, relaxed balance of breath support, vocal fold vibration, and appropriate voice resonance. Your natural voice appears to be the real you. Each of us has our own distinctive voices, which we can call our voice "fingerprint."

Your Voice "Fingerprint"

Just like a fingerprint, the human voice and speech pattern is amazingly distinctive. This is why a few words spoken on the smartphone by someone you know, or hearing a friend or family member talking, is all we need to identify who is speaking. Or we can quickly identify well-known celebrities or politicians by the sound of their speech and voice.

Our voice fingerprints are composed of a number of speech-voice behaviors that act separately or in combination. Here are the contributing parts of the voice "fingerprint":

> **The Number of Words You Say on One Breath.** Some of us say few words on one breath. Some say many. The relative amount of pausing or phrasing that you use becomes unique to you.

> **How Fast You Speak.** The normal conversational speaking rate is about 150 syllables per minute. If you speak at a different rate, this shapes the way you sound to others.

> **Your Rhythm of Speech.** Both the number of words you say per breath and your speed of talking contribute to

your speech rhythm (or prosody). The melody and speech accents you use in talking, your voice inflections, are distinctively your own.

Your Ease in Breathing. Some of us struggle to have enough breath when we speak. Others never seem to run out of air. Such habitual breathing patterns contribute to your vocal identity.

The Pitch of Your Voice. Pitch varies from person to person, even among people of the same age and sex. How high or low your voice is pitched is a major factor in distinguishing your voice from other voices.

The Loudness of Your Voice. Loudness, of course, varies according to the situation in which you speak, but some people normally speak louder, or softer, than others. Your loudness level is also part of your vocal identity.

The Relative Relaxation or Tension of Your Voice. How relaxed or tense you are shows in your voice. The way we sound reflects not only any special circumstances we are in, but also our psychological state.

Your Mood State. Vocal individuality also is influenced by such things as whether we are happy or sad, eager, bored, worried, or optimistic.

The Clarity of Your Speech Articulation. Distinctness of speech, or articulation, varies widely from person to person. Some people have distinct accents or dialects. Some have small or large articulation problems, such as not being able to say the *r* sound correctly, or they may have a lisp. Differences of articulation are one of the most noticeable behaviors that distinguish our speech from that of others.

The Resonance of Your Voice. The sound of the voice is heavily influenced by vocal resonance. The position of your tongue, your mouth opening, and shutting off your mouth from your nose continually change as you speak, which adds to your individual sound.

All of these speech-voice behaviors blend together, and what comes out is distinctively you, your individual voice. That is why you can say three words on the telephone and be recognized immediately.

But are you happy with that voice? Ask yourself these three critical questions:

1. Are you pleased with your own voice?
2. When you hear yourself on a recording or answering machine, do you like the way you sound?
3. Generally, do you think your voice makes a good impression on other people?

If the answer to any of these questions is "no," then by following a few suggestions in this book and by developing your natural voice through practice, you can become happier with the way you sound and sound better to others.

The Listen to Voices Test

The first step for improving your voice is to develop an awareness of different voices and how they compare with your own. That is the purpose of The Listen to Voices Test.

This six-step test is designed to develop an awareness of different voice characteristics. The test begins with an alphabetical list of 100 adjectives, or descriptors, of different voices (Table 1-1). Each word denotes a positive (+) or negative (−) opinion of a voice. For example, *clear* denotes a normal voice free of any kind of defect and is a positive (+) descriptor. The word *scratchy* is a negative descriptor. Some of these terms you will already have heard used to describe voices. Many such words are seldom used by any of us. And others have their own private meanings for different people.

1. Review the list of 100 word-descriptors. Take time to think about the meaning of each word. Then look at each word and judge it as positive (+) or negative (−), and mark it in the space before each word. Mark even those you are not too sure about. Even if you have never really thought much about voices before, this exercise will help you develop a better awareness of voice characteristics.

Table 1–1. 100 Word-Descriptors for Voice

___ 1. Abrasive	___ 35. Golden	___ 68. Powerful
___ 2. Affected	___ 36. Good	___ 69. Quiet
___ 3. Aged	___ 37. Gravelly	___ 70. Quivering
___ 4. Angry	___ 38. Happy	___ 71. Relaxed
___ 5. Baby	___ 39. Harmonious	___ 72. Resigned
___ 6. Bad	___ 40. Harsh	___ 73. Resonant
___ 7. Beautiful	___ 41. Heavy	___ 74. Rich
___ 8. Breathy	___ 42. High	___ 75. Ringing
___ 9. Bright	___ 43. Hoarse	___ 76. Rough
___ 10. Brilliant	___ 44. Hollow	___ 77. Sad
___ 11. Bubbly	___ 45. Husky	___ 78. Scratchy
___ 12. Cello-like	___ 46. Immature	___ 79. Sexy
___ 13. Chesty	___ 47. Insecure	___ 80. Shallow
___ 14. Clangy	___ 48. Intimidating	___ 81. Sharp
___ 15. Clear	___ 49. Joyful	___ 82. Silken
___ 16. Coarse	___ 50. Light	___ 83. Smooth
___ 17. Confident	___ 51. Lovely	___ 84. Sophisticated
___ 18. Constricted	___ 52. Low	___ 85. Stentorian
___ 19. Cool	___ 53. Macho	___ 86. Strident
___ 20. Covered	___ 54. Masculine	___ 87. Sultry
___ 21. Cutting	___ 55. Mature	___ 88. Thin
___ 22. Dark	___ 56. Mellow	___ 89. Throaty
___ 23. Decisive	___ 57. Melodious	___ 90. Tight
___ 24. Deep	___ 58. Metallic	___ 91. Timid
___ 25. Dry	___ 59. Monotone	___ 92. Tired
___ 26. Dull	___ 60. Nasal	___ 93. Ugly
___ 27. Effeminate	___ 61. Nervous	___ 94. Unsure
___ 28. Edgy	___ 62. Normal	___ 95. Velvety
___ 29. Fearful	___ 63. Old	___ 96. Warm
___ 30. Flat	___ 64. Open	___ 97. Wavering
___ 31. Feminine	___ 65. Pinched	___ 98. Wet
___ 32. Fluttering	___ 66. Pleasing	___ 99. Whining
___ 33. Forced	___ 67. Poor	___ 100. Whiskey
___ 34. Friendly		

2. Now turn to the last page of this chapter and compare your plus or minus markings with mine (Table 1–2). There are no right or wrong answers. When I made up the list of descriptors we ended up with more negative words (such as sad) than positive (such as happy).

3. See if you can apply some of these word-descriptors to the voices you may have heard on radio, television, or in movies. Selecting the words that might apply to a well-known voice can help you listen more critically to the voices around you. Go through the list below and apply the words you think describe the voice of each celebrity. I have listed my choices of six or seven descriptors for each person. Do you agree or disagree with my word choices?

- *Tom Brokaw:* aged, confident, low, masculine, resonant, throaty
- *Bill Clinton:* breathy, confident, friendly, hoarse, rough, tired, warm
- *Hillary Clinton:* clear, confident, feminine, mature, warm, wavering
- *James Earl Jones:* clear, deep, low, melodious, powerful, resonant
- *John McCain:* confident, decisive, hoarse, intimidating, old, strident
- *Marilyn Monroe:* affected, breathy, feminine, relaxed, sexy, sultry, wet
- *Barack Obama:* clear, confident, low, mellow, open, resonant, smooth
- *Meryl Streep:* bright, clear, cool, pleasing, sharp, warm

My descriptors for the voices of these well-known people may differ from yours. That would be predicted. The important part of this exercise is to apply descriptive labels to help you become more aware of the different sounding voices around you. And the same voice may differ in the way it sounds throughout the day and the circumstances surrounding the person.

Now, what about your own voice?

4. Listen to your own voice. Record your own voice when reading a page or when speaking aloud several sentences. As you

listen to the playback, select from the list of 100 descriptors seven or eight words that you think best describe your voice. Then listen to the playback again, and narrow your list down to three descriptors. These three words label your voice as you hear it, and how you think that other people may be making judgments about how you sound.

5. Ask a close friend, or your spouse, to review the 100-word list, and then select the seven or eight words he or she thought best describes your voice. Were any of your three descriptors among those selected by this other person? In Chapter 7, we'll see how these voice descriptors chosen by you and another close person relate to what might help you with your own voice.

6. Select five or six other voices that you may have heard online, radio, or TV. If possible, record these individual's voices and listen to the playback critically. Now, select a few words from the 100-word list that seem to best label each of the voices.

By completing the six steps above, you should start to become more aware of the individuality of the voices around you. You will certainly develop a better awareness of your own voice. And you will develop a better appreciation of those qualities of voices that are pleasing to hear and an awareness of those negative qualities of voice that are unpleasant.

How Can We Develop a Natural Normal Voice?

Up until now in this book, we mention both the natural and the normal voice. Over the years I have looked for a clear definition of the "natural voice"—and I have never found one that distinguishes it from what we call the "normal voice." Each of us has a natural, normal voice that is continually changing by the influence of our emotions, our physical state, and the situations in which we find ourselves. Most of the time our voices sound the same to the people around us. The natural voice is produced by a natural balance of breathing, phonation (the sound the vocal folds make when they are vibrating), and resonance.

In the following chapters we will show you different ways to find the natural voice that is distinctively your own. We will show you how to develop and maintain good voice and tell you what to do to avoid a bad voice, even in stressful situations.

In Chapter 2, we need to review some of the basic mechanisms we use to produce a better sounding voice.

Table 1–2. Author's Ratings of 100 Word-Descriptors for Voice

− 1. Abrasive	+ 35. Golden	+ 68. Powerful
− 2. Affected	+ 36. Good	+ 69. Quiet
+ 3. Aged	− 37. Gravelly	− 70. Quivering
− 4. Angry	+ 38. Happy	+ 71. Relaxed
− 5. Baby	+ 39. Harmonious	− 72. Resigned
− 6. Bad	− 40. Harsh	+ 73. Resonant
+ 7. Beautiful	− 41. Heavy	+ 74. Rich
+ 8. Breathy	+ 42. High	+ 75. Ringing
+ 9. Bright	− 43. Hoarse	− 76. Rough
+ 10. Brilliant	− 44. Hollow	− 77. Sad
+ 11. Bubbly	− 45. Husky	− 78. Scratchy
+ 12. Cello-like	− 46. Immature	+ 79. Sexy
− 13. Chesty	− 47. Insecure	− 80. Shallow
− 14. Clangy	− 48. Intimidating	− 81. Sharp
+ 15. Clear	+ 49. Joyful	+ 82. Silken
− 16. Coarse	+ 50. Light	+ 83. Smooth
+ 17. Confident	+ 51. Lovely	+ 84. Sophisticated
− 18. Constricted	+ 52. Low	+ 85. Stentorian
+ 19. Cool	+ 53. Macho	− 86. Strident
− 20. Covered	+ 54. Masculine	+ 87. Sultry
− 21. Cutting	+ 55. Mature	− 88. Thin
− 22. Dark	+ 56. Mellow	− 89. Throaty
+ 23. Decisive	+ 57. Melodious	− 90. Tight
+ 24. Deep	− 58. Metallic	− 91. Timid
− 25. Dry	− 59. Monotone	− 92. Tired
− 26. Dull	− 60. Nasal	− 93. Ugly
− 27. Effeminate	− 61. Nervous	− 94. Unsure
− 28. Edgy	+ 62. Normal	+ 95. Velvety
− 29. Fearful	+ 63. Old	+ 96. Warm
− 30. Flat	+ 64. Open	− 97. Wavering
+ 31. Feminine	− 65. Pinched	− 98. Wet
− 32. Fluttering	+ 66. Pleasing	− 99. Whining
− 33. Forced	− 67. Poor	− 100. Whiskey
+ 34. Friendly		

CHAPTER 2

Basic Mechanisms Needed for a Normal Voice

"Your voice problem may not be your fault,
but not doing anything about it—IS."

We are looking at a book like this to improve the way we speak and to use a better voice. For a lifetime most of us use the same voice, regardless of the situations in which we find ourselves, regardless of whether it pleases us or others, and regardless of whether it gives an accurate impression of who we really are. We take our voices for granted, as something like the shape of our nose or the size of our feet. As one patient said to me, "I've had this lousy voice all of my life, and no one ever told me that I could change it." But we will see in the chapters ahead, how some directed voice self-practice can improve the way we sound.

There is no magic required. Developing a voice that sounds better requires us to learn to use our breathing mechanisms, our vocal folds (sometimes called "vocal cords"), and our resonating structures in a coordinated easy voice. This natural voice is there waiting to be used. The natural voice requires a balance between the basic mechanisms required for breathing, phonation, and resonance. This voice balance is produced by the right amount of airflow to set the vocal folds into vibration; the sound this vibration produces is then resonating in the chest, the open cavities of the throat, the mouth, and the nasal cavities above.

Before we look at these three voice components (breathing, phonation, resonance) in greater detail, we need to consider how our emotions color the sound of our voices. All normal voices generally reflect how you feel inside. If you are happy, you sound happy. If you are angry or sad, your listeners may hear it in the sound of your voice. In most situations our voices *should* reveal how we feel. But certainly not in all situations. For example, an airline captain facing a difficult landing cannot let the passengers hear any fear in his or her voice. Or CEOs who may feel great tensions when making an important presentation do not want their voices to show any anxiety.

There are times then, when we must control our natural voice so that it represents us the way we want to appear, rather than the way we may feel inside. Parents do this frequently with their children. It is called voice control. In addition to developing a natural normal voice (the basic message of this book), we will also consider ways to control the natural voice in certain situations, such as on the phone or when suffering from stage fright or stress.

Back to the three mechanisms of voice: respiration, phonation, and resonance. How does each contribute to the normal voice?

Respiration (Breathing) and the Natural Voice

All voice and speech is produced on expiratory airflow. When we speak or sing, we take in a quick momentary breath and then let it out slowly. The outgoing air sets our vocal folds into vibration-producing voice. However, the body's need for oxygen renewal will always take priority over our wanting to talk. For example, if we are climbing a mountain trail, we will speak in short gasps despite our efforts to speak a longer sentence. Or, if we are involved in a tense situation, such as an auto accident, the brain will signal for more oxygen for the emergency, and our normal voice and speech may be compromised—sometimes, one can hardly speak.

In most situations, we have enough outgoing air for speech and voice. When we start to run out of air as we are speaking, we need to take a momentary pause in our speech. During the pause our chest expands again, we take in a new breath, and we are able to continue speaking. The muscle movements in the breath cycle take care of themselves automatically during the time of the pause. Also, the loudness of your voice is controlled by your breathing. A whisper, light voice requires very little outgoing air. The louder one's voice, the more air we use.

We breathe air in by a simple process: when the lungs need new air, the diaphragm (5 in Figure 2–1) contracts down and some chest muscles contract, increasing the space within the lungs; the air within the lungs is reduced in pressure allowing

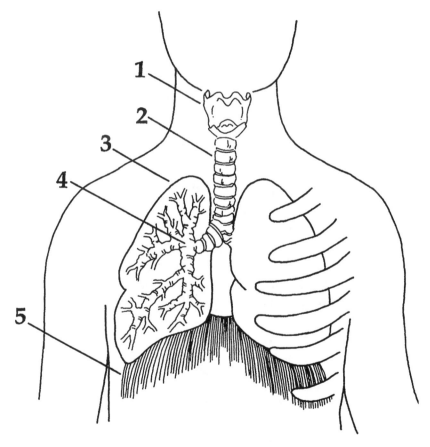

Figure 2–1. Breathing Mechanisms. Air from the nose and mouth passes through the larynx (1), through the windpipe or trachea (2), and into the lungs (3). The air is distributed through the lungs via the bronchial tubes (4). The large diaphragm (5), which separates the chest from the abdomen, is the primary muscle of inspiration.

the outside air to come in. When the diaphragm relaxes it rises, increasing the air pressure within. The exhaled air continues flowing out until the atmospheric air pressure is greater than the pressure within the lungs. The in and out breath cycle repeats itself for the next breath.

The key to breathing in and out for a natural voice is to do it effortlessly. For conversational speech, most of us require no special training in breathing. Contrary to what some people believe, we do not have to be trained in diaphragmatic breathing to develop a good speaking voice. Instruction in deep diaphragmatic breathing is necessary for the stage actor without amplification or for the jazz trombone player—but not for the average speaker. All we need to do is become aware of how many words we can say with average loudness on one breath. We need to pause before we get to this upper limit of words per breath, and the body will renew the breath it needs to continue speaking. As we shall see in Chapter 5, there are some easy ways to take in a good quick breath and learn to let it out slowly to support our voice.

Phonation (Voicing) and the Natural Voice

The outgoing airstream passes out of the lungs, via the bronchial tubes and the trachea then through the larynx (these structures are seen in Figure 2–1). The two vocal folds are two muscles covered by a membrane that sit side by side in the larynx. As we see in Figure 2–2, the two vocal folds are usually in one of two positions.

In sketch A, we see the two folds apart, like an inverted V. This is the open position they are in during breathing; the air passes between them without obstruction. For phonation, they come gently together as seen in sketch B. In this closed position, the outgoing airflow passes between them and sets them in vibration. As they vibrate, the vocal folds produce a noise that voice scientists and speech pathologists call phonation. We know it better as voice.

The normal voice can be produced only when the vocal folds are gently together. If they are too far apart, the voice is likely to be breathy. Vocal folds that are held together too tightly result

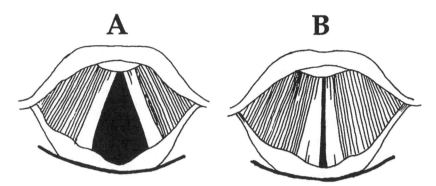

Figure 2–2. The Vocal Folds (often called vocal cords). **A.** The two vocal folds are apart in an inverted V position. **B.** The two vocal folds are together ready to begin voicing (phonation) when the outgoing airflow sets them into vibration.

in a harsh voice. A gentle proximity of the vocal folds produces the desired easy voice. You probably already produce it now and then. For example, when you say "uhm huh," this gentle sound of agreement is probably your natural voice, easy and relaxed.

The pitch of your voice is determined by the thickness, size, and tension of your vocal folds. Large, relaxed vocal folds produce low pitches. Thin, tense vocal folds produce high pitches. We cannot voluntarily change the shape of our vocal folds. We don't need to. As we speak, and certainly as we sing, the vocal folds constantly change size and tension. The muscles in the larynx and the vocal folds, which are a pair of muscles themselves, contract or relax automatically to produce the pitch we want to use.

The natural pitch of the voice, that easy "uhm huh" sound, can be produced with very little effort. It seems to exist several notes above the bottom of our total range. This natural pitch level is an important part of our natural voice, and we will talk about it in detail in Chapter 7.

Resonance and the Normal Voice

The resonance of the voice is produced primarily in the cavities above the vocal folds: the throat, mouth, and nose. The primary resonance cavity is the pharynx, or throat. The lateral and posterior walls of the throat are sphincteric muscles. When they contract, the pharynx becomes smaller (as it does singing on a high note). When these constrictor muscles relax, the pharynx becomes larger (as in using a low voice). A natural voice seems to require an open, relaxed throat.

Much voice resonance also occurs in the mouth. The position of the tongue in the mouth has a great deal of influence on how we sound. We talk in Chapter 8 about the effects on voice by the placement of the tongue within the mouth. A tongue that is carried far forward in the mouth can produce a baby-like voice. A backward carriage of the tongue produces a back focus to the voice, altering one's resonance to sound almost like the television character Alf. A vocal coach in New York City told me that a voice with good resonance sounds as if "it's coming right off the surface of the tongue in the middle of the mouth."

Only three sounds in English, *m, n, ng,* require nasal resonance. Nasal resonance is produced by sound waves traveling into the nasal cavities. The mouth and nasal cavities are separated by the boney hard palate (the front roof of the mouth) and the muscular soft palate (the back roof of the mouth). In normal speech, without *m, n,* or *ng,* the soft palate door to the nasal cavities remains closed. When we say the nasal sounds, this door quickly opens, by dropping down. The sound waves then have to travel through the soft palate door into the nasal cavities. As we will discuss in Chapter 9, some of us have too much nasal resonance, and some of us have too little. The natural voice has the right balance between oral and nasal resonance.

How to Tell if You Have a Voice Problem

A voice *disorder* is not the same as a voice problem. By a voice disorder we mean something that needs to be treated by a specialist. A conservative estimate of the percentage of voice disorders in adults is that about three percent of the population in this country over age 18 has a voice disorder of some kind. Some of the specialists listed in Chapter 16 are the best qualified professionals to help these seven million Americans with voice disorders.

But probably 25% of the adult population, although they do not have real voice disorders, are displeased with the way they sound and with the way their voices affect their careers and social lives. Their problems undoubtedly are with one or more of the elements of a natural voice that we have been discussing. Based on recent Census figures (U.S. Census, 2010) with a U.S. population of just over 320 million people, that means that about 80 million people have some concern about their voices. Take a few moments to find how your voice may be affecting your life. We have included for your use the Voice Handicap Index-10 (VHI-10, Rosen & others, 2004) that will help you in your self-evaluation (Table 2–1).

Table 2–1. The Voice Handicap Index 10 (VHI-10)

Instructions: These are statements that many people have used to describe their voices and the effects of their voices on their lives. Circle the response that indicates how frequently you have the same experience.					
0 = Never 1 = Almost Never 2 = Sometimes 3 = Almost Always 4 = Always					
1. My voice makes it difficult for people to hear me.	0	1	2	3	4
2. People have difficulty understanding me in a noisy room.	0	1	2	3	4
3. My voice difficulties restrict personal and social life.	0	1	2	3	4
4. I feel left out of conversations because of my voice.	0	1	2	3	4
5. My voice problem causes me to lose income.	0	1	2	3	4
6. I feel as though I have to strain to produce voice.	0	1	2	3	4
7. The clarity of my voice is unpredictable.	0	1	2	3	4
8. My voice problem upset me.	0	1	2	3	4
9. My voice makes me feel handicapped.	0	1	2	3	4
10. People ask, "What's wrong with your voice?"	0	1	2	3	4
Total: ____/40					

After administering this test to a number of adults, I was able to rate the degree of concern about voice on the following scale:

Number of True Answers	*Amount of Concern*
0–6	No concern
7–12	Mild concern
13–20	Moderate concern
21 or more	Severe concern

The higher your degree of concern, the more probable it is that you are using a voice that is different from your natural voice.

If you are concerned about your voice, you can now do something about it. For example, in the following chapter, you will discover some emotional, environmental, and/or physical factors that may be working against you from having a better voice. Once these problems are identified, you will learn what to do to decrease the impact they may be having on your voice. As you will soon see, learning to use an easy voice is not that difficult.

CHAPTER 3

Enemies of a Natural Voice

"Some situations seem to give my voice a lot of trouble."

In this chapter, we look at possible emotional, environmental, and physical enemies to having a better voice. You may not be able to eliminate them entirely, but when you encounter them, you need to know how to minimize their possible negative impact on your voice.

Emotional Enemies of a Natural Voice

We show our emotions in our voices. This is why we can hear someone we know well speak a few words on the phone, and we can make an instant judgment as to how well he or she is feeling. Many of the words on the 100 Word-Descriptor list you saw in Chapter 1 are adjectives describing the impact that emotion brings to the sound of our voice. We will first look at the typical effects some emotions have on voice. We will talk about ways to reduce these emotional affects on our voices in many coming chapters in this book. Among emotional enemies of a natural voice, here are five emotions that influence the way we sound:

1. Fearful: "choked up," shortness of breath, higher pitch, loudness changes

2. Angry: lower pitch, louder, longer phrases ending in lower pitch
3. Happy: good breath support, loudness meets situation needs, relaxed
4. Intimidating: "choked up," poor airflow, higher pitch, clenched teeth
5. Nervous: shortness of breath, higher pitch, hoarseness, throat clearing

Fearful. The body's overall response to fearful situations is to curb normal body function with a "run from the tiger" response. People who report being scared often say that they become all "choked up." That is, they feel the muscles in the throat tense up, shutting off their breath supply. Extreme fear can shut down one's ease of in and out breathing with the primary closing point being the valving action of the vocal folds, closing so tightly together that normal airflow is obstructed. In most fearful situations, however, the airflow is not completely shut off but reduced enough to make normal voice impossible.

Fear may also cause an elevation of the larynx, rising higher in the neck similar to where it is when one swallows. In this position, there is usually an elevation of voice pitch with some compromise in overall voice resonance. We look at ways to minimize the effects of fear on the voice in Chapters 10, 11, and 15. The most prominent method appears to be the yawn-sigh, which has the effect of lowering the larynx and opening up the airway.

Angry. Although everyone occasionally gets angry, there are certain situations where one is better hiding his or her anger, rather than letting it be heard. The animal response to respond angrily to situations has been usually conditioned out of us as children. Yet, now and then we do speak with anger in our voice. The angry voice is usually a louder voice with a lower voice pitch, even dropping in pitch toward the end of a sentence. This glide toward a lower voice is the voice of authority and at certain times, the voice is used well for negative discipline.

There are primarily two consequences for using an angry voice. First, we want others to know that we are angry. The angry voice carries its own message, often more apparent than the words we are using in our angry voice. Secondly, there are situations where we do not want our listeners to know that we are angry as we speak. Although we speak about angry voice management in future chapters, a first obvious way is not to speak. Take a moment or two to not show your anger. Whatever mental hygiene techniques one uses in life, this is a good time to use them. From a voice viewpoint, speaking in a quieter voice level, with a slightly higher pitch level, appears to soften the anger in one's voice.

Happy. We sound happy when we speak with a smile on our face. Our breath supply provides the amount of air we need to say what we want to say. The jaw and facial muscles are relaxed, which gives the lining of the resonance structures a softer surface, which gives voice resonance a "softer" sound. The lips and tongue are relaxed, freely able to play their role in speech articulation. For some people, particularly women, there may be a greater use of elevated voice pitches sounding in their spontaneous speech. Happiness, reflected in the voice, shows a voice that goes where the speaker wants it to go.

For any of us, a happy voice is a blessing to have most of the time. Obviously, such a voice is inappropriate in many situations: a job interview, giving directions, speaking at a funeral, testifying in court, and so forth. Each of us needs to be aware of the sound of our voices in certain situations.

Intimidating. Although people rarely find themselves in intimidating circumstances, when they do it can have devastating effects on one's voice. Breathing changes are often the most obvious thing one experiences with a shutting down of airflow. Survivors of such threatening events tell us that they felt their throats "choked up," making it almost impossible to respond with their normal voice. One sounds intimidated (even if he or she is not) with some elevation of voice pitch and barely audible speech.

If one is required to answer some kind of intimidating question, the response should be delayed. By using the invisible yawn-sigh (described in Chapter 11) some vocal tract relaxation can be achieved. The larynx is then lowered, breathing is restored, and a soft voice can be produced.

Nervous. Most people can experience nervousness in some situations. Sometimes a nervous response can appear beyond the control of the person. A common example of this is the "doctor's office" syndrome when measuring blood pressure; at rest, and not knowing that blood pressure is being taken, the individual displays normal pressure. However, wearing the cuff in the doctor's office, his blood pressure is measured as quite elevated.

Different people react to the stresses around them in different ways. Some folks may stand up at a meeting and speak their views without any apparent nervousness. Others in the same situation would prefer to stay quiet and not reveal their nervousness when speaking in public. The nervous voice, also, seems to only occur in certain situations.

The nervous voice usually shows some shortness of breath when trying to speak. There is usually some hoarseness with some elevation of voice pitch. There may be excessive throat clearing as the person tries to find his or her normal voice. The treatment of the nervous voice is twofold: (1) with counseling and possible medication, it may be possible to decrease nervousness sensitivity, and (2) voice can be helped following the exercises in this book in the search for the natural, normal voice.

Environmental Enemies of a Natural Voice

Among many environmental enemies of a natural voice, here are five common ones:

1. Air quality: dust, fumes, smoke, smog
2. Special circumstances: phones, microphones, cars, planes, public speaking
3. Humidity: low or high moisture levels in the air you breathe
4. Noise: recreational, occupational, travel, extraneous noises
5. Speaker-listener distance: too close, too far, large room, outside speaking

Air Quality Problems. The most common air quality problem is not smog, but dust. Dust from chalk, the carpet, household dust, backstage dust, outside dust blown into your home or office from passing cars, construction projects, leaf blowers.

Dust is an irritant to your airway, the wet or moist linings of your nose, throat, and vocal folds. When irritated, these air passages may become red and swollen, often causing a change in the pitch and quality of your voice.

Indoor dusting can do wonders to reduce this problem. I remember an actress telling me, "After they started wet-mopping the stage and backstage floors before the show, my voice problems disappeared."

Do what you can to reduce the dust in your home, office, or other work places. Although you cannot eliminate outside dust sources beyond your control, it can be reduced around your home by plantings and by watering down dusty areas. In some foreign countries, such as Spain and Italy, during the dry, dusty months of summer, you can see shopkeepers and homeowners sprinkling water on the sidewalks in front of their shops and homes to keep down the dust.

The smog in our cities from the emissions of cars, trucks, buses, and industry and the smoke from fireplaces and barbecues are definite irritants to anyone's airway.

Inside the house or work place, air conditioning can make a big difference. Air conditioning units in cars are perhaps more important for their air filtering properties than for their cooling. A drugstore salesman in Los Angeles cured his chronic hoarseness by adding an air conditioning unit to his car.

Become more aware of air quality as a potential enemy of your voice. If bad air is present, drink more fluids, stay indoors more, and see if you can add air conditioning to your living and work spaces.

Special Circumstances. There are certain common situations that seem to work against having a natural voice, and they vary from individual to individual. Some people have difficulty using their natural voice on the telephone. Because so many people have a voice problem using the phone, we have included a separate chapter (Chapter 12) on this topic. In that chapter, we also talk about how to keep your natural voice when using a smartphone, microphone, house phone, or when wearing earbuds or earphones.

Some people find that talking before groups, or speaking with a supervisor, can have a negative effect on their voices. Chapters 10 through 14 contain tips for situations like these.

Automobiles and airplanes are common places where people have voice problems, not only because such environments are noisy but because they can be excessively dry. On long car trips, we should avoid protracted conversations and carry a supply of soft drinks or water. Airplane cabins are also often too dry, and good fluid intake (avoiding alcohol) during air travel helps prevent not only jet lag, but voice problems as well. These concerns are of particular importance to people who are expected to speak at the end of a long journey, perhaps at a conference or meeting, in a lecture or workshop, or during a sales call.

Humidity. Too low or too high humidity can be an enemy of your natural voice. An ideal humidity for the voice is between 30% and 40%. In desert areas, such as Tucson or Palm Springs, humidity levels frequently drop below 10%. This dries out the air passages in the vocal tract. The mucosal surfaces of the mouth and throat become excessively dry, often showing red streaks or inflammation. In such circumstances, we need to drink far more fluids and add moisture to the air. Inside, humidity can be raised by swamp coolers, humidifiers, and by keeping well-watered house plants around.

Humidity levels above 80% may add too much moisture to our airways, which can cause us to continually clear our throats and blow our noses. In cars, homes, and offices, excessive humidity can be controlled somewhat by using air conditioners and furnaces that have dehumidifiers. Unfortunately, many of these units remove too much moisture from the air. Humidity levels around 30% to 40% seem to be best for the voice. Most hardware stores sell gauges that can show humidity as well as temperature levels.

Noise. Some people call noise the biggest air pollutant of all. And often, the sources of smog and dust, cars, construction projects, blowers are also sources of noise pollution.

In everyday life, we frequently find ourselves in noisy places: in cars, planes, trains, buses, subways, restaurants, bars, discos, stadiums, around power mowers and blowers, construction sites, or just on the sidewalks of a busy city street. We need to be concerned about prolonged speaking in such circumstances. When we speak in a noisy situation, generally we are unaware of how loudly we are talking. Many of us have had the experience of having music, or conversation, stop suddenly when we were talking. We are surprised to find that we were almost shouting.

The extra effort required to speak in noisy environments involves using more air for a louder voice, a higher pitch, and greater precision in enunciation. This can severely tax our vocal equipment and prevent us using our natural voices.

One noisy situation worth special mention is wearing headphones. Avoid using your voice much when listening through your headset. The noise level is usually too high for you to speak at your preferred normal level.

Speaker-Listener Distance. Most of us use many different voices every day, depending on how near or far we are to our listeners. At close distances, we speak at a low loudness level.

When we stand before a group, our listeners are farther away, and we need to take a bigger breath to speak loudly and to use fewer words per breath.

For a good voice, and one that can be heard effectively, we need to vary our loudness to meet the situation and avoid using the same loudness level wherever we are. In Chapter 6, Loud Enough or Too Loud?, we will look at ways to find the loudness levels appropriate for various speaker-listener distances.

Physical Enemies of a Natural Voice

In addition to environmental threats to the natural voice, there are some physical factors that influence how we sound. The eight conditions listed below may be enemies of developing and using your natural voice.

1. Aging: The voice changes throughout our lifespan.
2. Allergies and infections: Common ailments change our voices.
3. Fatigue: Tiredness quickly shows in our voices.
4. Fear: Being afraid affects our airway.
5. Hormonal changes: Glandular changes influence the voice.
6. Hydration: Moisture levels in the airway and the vocal tract affect the voice.
7. Medications: Some medicines may have impact on the voice.
8. Recreational drugs: Smoking, alcohol, and illegal drugs have an impact on our voices.

Aging. Voice mirrors physical growth and other changes of the body. At age 8, boys and girls basically have the same voice pitch, near middle C on a musical scale. With the advent of puberty, the male voice drops an octave, and the female voice half an octave. A man's voice continues to deepen as he gets older, until past age 70 when his voice pitch begins to elevate slightly. The adult female voice tends to get lower in pitch with each successive decade. In very old age, past age 90, the voice pitches of men and women are relatively similar.

As we get older, our rate of speech also generally slows a bit from the 150 words a minute of our younger days. An older man once asked me, "How can I sound younger?" I told him, "Listen to Bob Hope. Here is a man in his nineties who uses a slightly higher pitch, and speaks rapidly, and this makes his speech patterns sound young."

Allergies and Infections. The professional user of voice (and this includes not just actors, singers, preachers, and teachers, but all of us who need to use our voices effectively in our daily work) is always fearful of an allergy or irritation that might temporarily put his or her voice out of commission.

For people with severe airway allergies, the swollen and inflamed membranes of the throat and nose can produce hoarseness and even complete loss of voice. The best source of treatment for allergies is a physician, either an allergist or an ear-nose-throat specialist. Be wary of taking over-the-counter allergy medications, such as antihistamines, on your own. Most antihistamines have profound drying effects on the larynx, which only add to the deterioration of voice.

Most throat infections are viral in origin and are difficult to treat. The best thing we can do when a severe cold affects our voice is to rest and take extra fluids, particularly citrus juices. If we sound hoarse, we should go on complete voice rest for a few days, using no voice at all. Talking a lot with a voice hoarse from a cold can damage the vocal folds. Voice rest will allow the infected vocal folds to heal. (If a severe head cold lingers more than seven days, you should see a doctor.)

Fatigue. We all know the symptoms of physical fatigue: we want to lie down, perhaps have a drink of some kind, and most of us want to be left alone. If we are forced to speak to someone, our voice is light, higher in pitch, and lower in volume than usual. At these times, it is not always possible to have the kind of voice you would like to have. Yet with rest and a proper diet, it is amazing how quickly your voice will come back. If you need to use your voice when fatigued, elevate your pitch a note and speak a bit faster. Adding a higher focus to your voice (see Chapter 8) can also make a fatigued voice sound more alive.

Fear. When we are afraid, the body alerts a number of physical systems to be ready to respond to danger. Our breathing rate increases, our heartbeat accelerates, our blood pressure goes up, the larynx tends to elevate, and the vocal folds often form a tight protective sphincter.

All of the above body postures help the body make a realistic response to a fearful situation. The problem is, however, that most of the time we don't need such forceful reactions. The voice gives out the sounds of fear. It sounds tense and has a higher pitch, and we say fewer words than normal per breath. In Chapter 11, Stage Fright and Other Fears, we talk about things we can do to take the sound of fear out of our voices; for example, a big yawn followed by a sigh can make our voice sound more relaxed.

Hormonal Changes. The dramatic voice changes in puberty experienced by both boys and girls are obvious evidence of the impact of sex hormones on the vocal tract and are normal. The adult male and female pitch levels stay about half an octave apart throughout most of life. However, the female may experience some special fluctuations in pitch (see Chapter 13, The Female Voice) during menstruation and after the menopause, as a direct result of normal hormonal changes.

There are some abnormal hormonal barriers to the natural voice. The adrenal glands can become underproductive, which can keep voice pitch at high, prepubertal levels, or overproductive, which can markedly lower voice pitch. Diseases of the pituitary glands can retard laryngeal growth. An inactive thyroid gland can lower pitch, give a low focus to the voice, and reduce normal loudness. Hyperthyroidism can result in rapid speech and elevated voice pitch. Pitch levels that are inappropriate for an individual's age and sex may be the result of some kind of hormonal imbalance. All such abnormal conditions are best identified and treated by an endocrinologist.

Hydration. Careful attention to moisture levels in both inspired air and the body is essential to a normal voice. Most of us need to drink more fluids, coffee, juice, tea, or soft drinks. A dry vocal tract will not function as well as a moist one. Fluids increase saliva and moisture in the airway, from your nostrils down to the bronchial tubes in your lungs. Also, the air that we breathe, as we noted earlier, should contain about 30% to 40% humidity to prevent vocal tract dryness.

Without adequate hydration, our voices sound strained and lack their normal resonance. The throat will not only feel dry, but there may be pain. With adequate intake of fluids, the sound of the voice can improve, and throat dryness and pain can disappear. Some performers increase their fluid intake before performance as a good way of maintaining adequate vocal tract moisture during performance. For the occasional person who suffers from excessive mouth dryness, there are several over-the-counter preparations that are helpful for increasing mouth saliva. Ask your pharmacist about them.

Medication. Among over-the-counter drugs, the primary enemies of the vocal tract are aspirin and antihistamines. Continuous and heavy use of aspirin can result in slight hemorrhaging of small blood vessels on the vocal folds, which can lower pitch and may produce some hoarseness. Antihistamines tend to dry the throat excessively and make prolonged speaking almost impossible.

Most prescription drugs will not hurt your voice. However, among those that can change your voice are the diuretics (frequently used by dieters), which can excessively dry the airway. Also, some drugs used in the treatment of hypertension to lower blood pressure can have drying effects. Some of the Beta-block drugs, which may be prescribed for heart problems, have voice-related side effects, such as throat spasms or sudden loss of voice. Prescription hormones can cause difficulty in breath control, pitch, and voice quality.

You need to be aware of the voice-changing side effects of prescription drugs. If you are taking such a drug, ask your physician or pharmacist about it. A serious user of voice should ask his or her physician about possible side effects of prescribed medications.

Recreational Drugs. Smoking is a primary enemy of developing a better voice. Cigarette, cigar, and pipe smoke have profound drying effects on the vocal tract, and the tars and irritants in the smoke often cause irritation of the mucosal linings of the air passages. Smoking can cause shortness of breath, throat clearing, lowering of voice pitch, and a decrease in voice loudness. After a habitual smoker stops smoking, many of these symptoms fortunately begin to clear up. It should be pointed out that many, but not all, mild-to-moderate smokers never experience any voice difficulties, but they are surely playing the wrong side of the odds.

Mild (one drink daily) to moderate (two to three drinks) use of alcohol does not seem to harm the natural voice. But heavy use (three or more drinks a day) acts as a vasodilator, enlarging the small blood vessels of the vocal folds, and can result in a husky or rough, low-pitched voice, the "whiskey tenor."

Among recreational drugs, marijuana, when smoked often, can have pronounced drying effects on the membranes of the throat and larynx. Cocaine can cause severe vasoconstriction (shrinking) of the membranes of the nose, resulting in changes of vocal resonance, such as in increased nasality.

Along with health and legal consequences, the serious user of voice should consider the potentially harmful effects on the voice from smoking, heavy use of alcohol, and use of illegal drugs such as marijuana or cocaine.

CHAPTER 4

You and Your Natural Voice

"We have met the enemy and he is us."
—Walt Kelly

The above quote from Walt Kelly's Pogo seems to apply to a great deal of human behavior, and voice production is no exception. Although the various factors we discussed in the last chapter can profoundly affect how well you speak, the biggest enemy of your natural voice is usually your own vocal behavior. Habitual misuse of vocal equipment invariably results in voice strain, and over a period of time, that strain may create voice problems.

The following simple descriptive list of poor vocal behaviors may help you identify the source of your own problems.

What You May Doing to Prevent a Natural Voice

- Clenched teeth: You speak through clenched teeth.
- Hard glottal attack: You use too much effort to speak.
- Loudness problems: You speak too loudly or too softly.
- Nasality: You speak through your nose too much.
- Pitch problems: Your voice is pitched too high or too low.
- Running out of air: You don't budget your air for speaking.
- Talk, talk, talk: You talk so much that your voice gets tired.

- Throat clearing: You clear your throat too often.
- Throat focus: You speak too low in your throat.
- Posture problems: You sit or stand improperly.
- Stressful environments: Under stress you make inappropriate demands on your voice.
- Misinformation: Poor information about your voice causes you to create, or persist in, voice problems.

Clenched Teeth. Every now and then you see someone who speaks with his teeth clenched together, using almost no jaw or lip movement, almost like a ventriloquist.

This clenched-teeth way of talking puts great strain on the vocal tract. It takes a lot of muscular effort to speak with such restricted mouth and jaw movements. Lack of mouth and jaw movement forces the tongue to do all the work. The voice comes out muffled, speech can be indistinct, and listeners can get the impression that the speaker is reluctant to communicate at all.

To counteract this, there are techniques that encourage jaw and lip movement, such as the open-mouth and yawn-sign exercises described in Chapters 10 and 11.

Hard Glottal Attack. The abruptness that we use when speaking is known as glottal attack. The glottis is the space between the vocal folds. Glottal attack is the term we use to describe how quickly the vocal folds close the glottal space. A soft glottal attack is heard in the easy speech of the true Southerner. Vowels are prolonged, and the overall speech pattern sounds easy and relaxed. The opposite speech pattern is a crisp, forceful (and frequently forced) way of speaking. Voice scientists and speech pathologists label this a *hard* glottal attack.

We hear the hard attack often in the big cities of the northeastern United States, or when we listen to many television interviewers and newscasters. It is a voice that sounds impersonal and, like the loud voice described below, can keep listeners at a distance. The hard glottal attack takes a toll on the voice, often causing vocal strain and hoarseness. Most of the subsequent chapters of this book give you techniques to eliminate hard glottal attack, if you have it.

Loudness Problems. The loudness of our voices should continually adjust to the changing noise levels around us, to the physical distance between us and our listeners, and to the social circumstances we are in. Unfortunately, many of us habitually use the same level of loudness, regardless of where we are, and consistently speak too loudly or too softly. An inappropriately loud voice can affront or intimidate listeners. The clarity of speech heard with the too-soft voice is often irritatingly indistinct.

You can change your voice loudness primarily by changing the amount of air you take in before you speak and by adjusting the number of words you say on that one breath. But there are many other loudness techniques that can be used, too. Chapter 6, Loud Enough or Too Loud?, describes exercises that will help a voice that is too soft or too loud.

Nasality. Another major speaking problem is a nasal-sounding voice. Some voices are so nasal that it is difficult to understand what is said. The problem seems aggravated when the speaker uses a public address system, and in places like hospitals and airports, a nasal voice can create listening difficulties. Also, nasal voices are simply irritating and can be yet another reason why people don't listen to what you say because of how you say it.

In many ways, a nasal voice is a voice with an excessively high focus. The focus is so high that it is in the nose. Because so many of our voices are too nasal, Chapter 9, Talking Through Your Nose, is devoted to techniques for reducing voice nasality.

Pitch Problems. The natural pitch level we use when we answer "uhm-huh" to someone we are talking with is usually near our natural pitch level. Many of us, however, customarily use a voice that is pitched higher or lower than that, and such a voice may be produced with some strain on the vocal tract.

Pitch is one of the major voice characteristics that establishes your vocal identity and personality. We are identified not only by our overall pitch level, but by the way we vary pitch within conversational passages—our pattern of speech inflections. A voice that is pitched too high or too low on the phone can cause the person on the other end of the line to think we are someone else, or even to be confused about what sex we are. A voice that doesn't use inflections is a monotonous, tiring voice, whereas an over inflected voice can be distracting and irritating to listeners.

Sometimes changing your pitch only one note up or down can add attractiveness and a relaxed sound to the way you speak.

For those who speak too softly, raising pitch one note can take the strain out of speaking loudly enough to be heard. And varying your pitch for inflected speech can make all the difference in whether people find what you say interesting or dull. The exercises presented in Chapter 7, The Well-Aimed Pitch, such as the "uhm-huh," can keep your listeners from responding, "ho hum."

Running Out of Air. Although it happens all the time, it doesn't make sense that a person runs out of breath when speaking. From the moment of birth, our breathing apparatus is totally automatic. Awake or asleep, when we need air, our bodies simply take it in, adjusting for situations when we need more air (exercising) and less air (sleeping). But when it comes to speaking, many of us try to become do-it-yourselfers. That makes about as much sense as crawling under the hood of your car and moving the engine pistons up and down by hand.

Voice is produced by outgoing breath. For speech, we take in a bit more air than we do for normal breathing. Problems arise when that first breath isn't big enough to sustain all the words we want to say. It is at this point that many of us seem to forget that the breathing process is automatic. We go on trying to speak, with a tight, strangled voice, or we start racing to the end of a sentence with our voice getting increasingly faint, when all we ever have to do is pause. For those of you with breathing problems, pause is the magic word. When you do, your body automatically takes in more air, your lungs fill again, and you are ready to speak more words in an easy, natural manner.

We talk about breathing for the speaking voice in the next chapter, To Breathe or Not To Breathe, and show you how to find out how many words you can comfortably say on one breath.

Talk, Talk, Talk. Some people never seem to stop talking. They act as if the sound of their voices is the only thing that keeps them visible to those around them. At the least, they more interested in what they say than in what anyone else might say. Sometimes we wonder if they even listen to themselves.

On the other hand, many of us are in occupations that require an enormous amount of talking: teachers, salespersons, air controllers, actors, announcers, telephone receptionists. More of us have occupations where we periodically need to do a great deal of talking, such as being called on to make presentations, demonstrate products or systems, or speak at meetings or conferences.

For all heavy users of voice, whether occasional or frequent, it is essential to speak in as natural a manner as possible. Poor voice behavior can cause strain and fatigue, which in turn produces voice symptoms that are unattractive, interfere with communication, and can give a false impression of you.

A strained or tired voice can be hoarse, lack volume (and conviction), and often may have unwanted changes in pitch. Worst of all, a tired voice can elicit similar negative reactions from listeners. If a speaker sounds tired, the audience feels tired. If a speaker's voice sounds strained, you can see strain in the audience too—restlessness, inattention, even irritation, or a "let's get this over with" reaction.

If your occupation requires you to talk a great deal, make a conscious effort to cut down on your talking during times when you don't need to speak, such as when you are by yourself, during meals, and away from work.

The parts of the body that produce voice are largely muscle. We use muscles to take in breath and to control letting it out. Muscles in the larynx and vocal folds produce the sounds of language. As with any other muscles, prolonged use tires them. So in speaking, as in other athletic situations, give yourself a voice break during your breaks.

All of the chapters in this book are designed to help you use each element of voice production (breathing, phonation, resonance) in a completely natural manner to lessen strain and fatigue.

Throat Clearing. When you clear your throat, the vocal folds rub tightly together as outgoing air violently passes between them. Over time, this can cause them to become irritated.

The irritated folds then exude more mucus to protect themselves. When we feel the presence of this mucus, we clear the throat again to get rid of it, and the problem repeats itself.

Some of us also clear our throats when we are ill at ease or as a way of getting attention. Often, it is a kind of announcement that we are about to speak, and reflects our anxiety over how our first words will sound. Throat clearing is often more of a habit than a way of getting rid of mucus on the vocal folds. It can be annoying for those listening to us. Worse than that, it can irritate the vocal folds enough to cause hoarseness.

For whatever reason that we do it, throat clearing should be a rare event. Instead, we recommend that you learn to swallow. If you feel that there is mucus in your throat, take an exaggerated and sudden sniff. This sudden inhalation will often dislodge any mucus on your vocal folds, which you can then swallow. (The normal person swallows quarts of throat mucus every day.)

Another technique for avoiding throat clearing is the silent cough. If you cough in a light but sudden whisper, this too will often dislodge vocal fold mucus, which can then be swallowed.

These tips are probably all you need if you have a throat-clearing habit, and we did not feel it was necessary to devote a chapter to this problem, even though it is a common one. One last word. If you do find it necessary to clear your throat from time to time, do it gently, not explosively. The kinder you are to your vocal folds, the kinder they will be to you over the years.

Throat Focus. Some people sound as if their voices come from deep down in their throats. Such a low throat focus often produces a voice pitch that is too low and a voice that is not loud enough. People who use a low voice focus often complain of losing their voices or of becoming hoarse after a lot of speaking. People who use an excessively high voice focus sound very nasal and complaints may come from people who have to listen to them.

With a normal focus, the voice sounds as if it is coming from the middle of the mouth, perhaps on the upper surface of the tongue. With this more vertical focus, you can usually use your voice all day long without developing any voice problems. As you listen to people who use their voices a lot—entertainers, actors, announcers, public speakers of all kinds—pay attention to where their voices seem to be coming from. These are people whose livelihood depends on good speaking habits, and they cannot afford to develop voice problems. Almost certainly you will hear that of most them focus their voices in the middle of their mouths.

We will look at voice focus in more detail in Chapter 8, Is Your Voice in Focus?, and give you exercises for developing the imagery for focusing your voice in the middle of your mouth.

Posture Problems. It may surprise many of you, but poor sitting and standing posture not only makes a bad visual impression, but can markedly interfere with producing a good voice. A typical poor sitting posture is the slouch: shoulders forward, abdomen protruded, and chin down. A slouched posture often contributes to a weak, ineffective voice. Such a position makes it difficult for the body to take in the air it needs for good speech. Try it. Try taking in a breath while slouched. Then try taking in a breath while sitting tall, with your back firmly against the back of your chair with your shoulders back. In the latter position, you should feel a deeper inspiration of air that makes it possible to complete your phrases and sentences with adequate volume and a natural-sounding voice. People with sedentary jobs, in particular, need to watch their posture. They can often improve the sound of their voices by keeping in mind the command: Sit tall.

A good standing posture, standing tall, is also important to a good voice. The standing slouch is just as common as the sitting slouch, and the results for speaking are the same. There is, however, no need for a stiff, military stance. All you have to do is keep your body erect but relaxed. A good standing posture can be practiced with your back to a wall. Your heels, buttocks, and shoulder blades should touch the wall, along with the back of your head.

Two bits of imagery can also help. First, imagine that the back top of your head is hanging by a rope from the ceiling. This will put your head at the right angle with your chin neither too high nor too low. Second, imagine that you have a large tail that you bring forward between your legs. This will help tilt your pelvis forward a bit, which in turn tucks in the abdomen.

These simple suggestions will help you not only sound better, but look better as well. If, however, you feel that you have a persistent posture problem that interferes with developing a good voice, you might want to consult a physiatrist (see Chapter 16) or a physical therapist. For most of us, however, the best posture for speaking is as easy as remembering what was said about sitting and standing tall.

Stressful Situations. All of the poor voice practices just discussed are commonly aggravated, or even initiated, by stress. Stress causes us to make unusual demands on our vocal equipment.

As we saw in the previous chapter, stress on voice can come from things such as pollution, infections, smoking, and dietary practices. It can also stem from anxiety in work, social, or recreational activities.

Anxiety reactions to stress can affect our voices in two ways. One, they can cause us to tax our voices because we need to speak longer, louder, or with more intensity than usual. Or two, anxiety may cause us to speak in a voice that is not our natural voice.

We are all familiar with the voice symptoms of anxiety: the dry throat and mouth, shortness of breath, changes in pitch, and all the things we associate with the term stage fright. In Chapter 10, Keeping Your Natural Voice Under Stress, we list 20 voice symptoms related to stress and show you techniques for overcoming them.

It is important to remember, however, that we are all "on stage" frequently in the course of our normal work and social lives. There are always times when you are called on to do something that is not routine, to give good or bad news or crucial information to those you work for or who work for you. In addition, many of us voluntarily subject ourselves to stressful situations in our recreations in team sports, amateur or semiprofessional singing and acting, even in informal social situations that suddenly turn formal when we are asked to say a few words or to offer or respond to a toast.

It is not possible, or perhaps even desirable, to remove all stress from our lives. It is possible, however, to minimize or eliminate stress symptoms from your voice when you feel the need to do so. To take some liberties from Rudyard Kipling's famous poem, "If you can keep your voice when all about you are losing theirs...," then you probably have used the helpful techniques we describe in Chapter 11, Stage Fright and Related Fears.

Misinformation. Many of us have received bad information about how voice is made, and why our voices sound the way they do. Some of us are chronically short of breath when we speak, because we learned somewhere that to get in adequate breath we need to work at it or to use diaphragmatic breathing. Or we have been told that our voice sounds best at the lowest pitch we can produce. Or that a loud voice makes us seem more confident, or that a soft voice is more appealing. Virtually any of the problems discussed earlier in this chapter can be caused or aggravated by bad information about voice production, which can make it difficult or impossible for you to remedy them.

However, the most common bit of misinformation we have about our voice is this: our voice is something we are born with, and whether it is pleasing to us or to others, there is nothing we can do to change it. That is a very unfortunate bit of misinformation for the roughly 80 million Americans who believe they have voice problems. The good news is that it is untrue. Most of us with voice problems have made our voices sound the way they do. We have learned bad voice habits and have persisted in using them.

What has been learned can be unlearned, and new voice practices can be developed that will give you a pleasing, natural voice. That is the essential message of this book. The following chapters will help you to identify specific voice problems and give you specific exercises to correct them. By replacing misinformation with good information, you will be able to find and use your natural voice.

CHAPTER 5

To Breathe or
Not to Breathe

"He had too many words for too little air."

Many people seem to have all the breath they need when they speak. Others seem to run out of air and struggle to finish what they say. Robert was a case where running out of air almost meant running out of gas in an otherwise accelerating career.

In his early 30s, Robert's life had started to take off. Not only was he getting new responsibilities and promotions at the insurance firm that employed him, but increasingly he was also being asked to take on civic duties in the community where he lived.

Conscientious as always, Robert began to devote new attention to self-improvement, taking pains with his clothes and grooming, and signing up for night classes. Because now he was asked to speak to groups, too, Robert thought it would be a good idea to get some experience in public speaking, and he joined the local chapter of a national speakers' organization. There he had his first serious setback. Although he had a lot to say about business and community affairs, his speaking voice was a handicap, not a help, in saying it.

Listeners had a hard time understanding Robert because he was a "fader." His sentences started out clear and strong enough, but his voice soon faded away and people kept asking, "What did he say?" After a while, they lost interest. By the end of his sentences, Robert sometimes was whispering.

When he came to us for help, I needed only to go to one of his speaking engagements to hear what the problem was. Robert often spoke as many as 25 words on one breath. It was too many words. He was literally running out of air before he finished a sentence.

We demonstrated to him that all he needed to do was pause every 15 words or so. When he paused, he took in a new breath without effort. By cutting down the number of words per breath, his voice was loud enough all the way through whatever he was saying. With some practice, Robert's serious setback soon turned out to be only a minor stumbling block in his rising career.

Posture and the Normal Voice

Before we begin practicing different things we can do to improve breath support for a better voice, we need to think again about our posture. Toward the end of the last chapter, Chapter 4, we presented some critical posture suggestions. We need to re-read them again. The best posture for a normal voice is sitting or standing erect with the individual remembering "to think tall." The ideal head position is produced by using the image of a rope from above attached to the upper back of the head. This places the head looking forward parallel to the floor, chin not looking down or upward, but looking straight ahead.

In recent years we have seen in our voice clinic a number of young people complaining about hoarseness. It seems that they are speaking many hours a day on smartphones or tablets, with their chins pointing down, almost touching the upper chest. This is consistent with what we observe with numerous students on our campuses looking down on their hand-held electronic devices as they walk and sit. This persistent chin-down posture (kyphosis) is reported by physical therapists as seen in an increase of neck-shoulder-upper back problems, requiring some physical relief by maintaining a normal head posture for greater time periods of the day. Likewise, for anyone wanting to improve his or her voice, voice improvement is more likely for those who keep a more level head position.

To Breathe or Not to Breathe

The miracle of breathing is that it is all done for us automatically from the moment we were born. When we need air for any kind of exertion, we automatically take in more and larger breaths. When we sleep, we don't need to instruct or monitor our breathing mechanism; it keeps working steadily and slowly.

All speech and singing is produced by the outgoing breath stream passing between the vocal folds, producing their vibration. Breathing for speech is accomplished by a quick inspiration (so fast we are unaware of it), followed by a prolonged expiration. The voice is powered by the strength of the outgoing breath.

We usually take in more breath than we need to use for speaking. Most of us, therefore, have ample air for speech, and experience little or no breathing strain while talking. All we have to do is think about what we want to say and begin saying it.

Yet many people who have normal breathing mechanisms, free of disease, find themselves short of breath when they speak. In some cases, the problem may be caused by simple anxiety, which can make breathing more rapid and shallower. If you think some of your breathing problems during speech come from anxiety and nervousness, in addition to reading this chapter, you should look carefully at Chapters 10 and 11 on stress and stage fright. For many other people the problem is that they do not use their normal breathing when speaking. Voice problems related to poor breath support can usually be helped by just letting it occur more naturally.

The body has a lot of vital processes that are completely automatic, from blinking to heartbeat, and breathing is one of them. You don't have to consciously direct your blinking to keep the surface of your eyes moist, or your heartbeat to keep blood pumping through your body. With breathing for speech, all you have to do is learn how to breathe (or relearn, because you were born knowing how) as naturally and easily when you speak as you do in the other activities of your life. The big difference for speech is that it requires a quick inspiration followed by a prolonged expiration, whereas for most of our other daily activities, inspiration and expiration are more nearly equal.

Breathing problems in speech can become habitual. They will often get worse unless the person who has them takes steps to correct them. It isn't hard. In the tests and exercises that follow we speak of breath control, but what you will actually be discovering is natural control over breathing: the right amount of breath, the right amount of words you can say on a breath, and how to do this easily, without effort or strain.

The Breath Control Test

You will need a stopwatch or a watch or clock with a second hand to take this test. After taking in a slightly larger than normal breath, measure the seconds that you can sustain your expiration for each of the following tasks:

1. Take in a breath and then make a hissing sound, *sssss*. There is no voice when we hiss. Sustain it as long as you can. After the first time, try prolonging the sound a few more times. Take the longest time and enter your score here: _____ seconds.
2. Take a breath and then count as far as you can as you exhale. After the first time, try a few times to count further. Time each attempt at counting. Take your longest time and enter your score here: _____ seconds.

Scoring the Breath Control Test

1. Prolonging the sssss. In general, larger people with larger rib cages can hold on to an expiration longer than smaller people. Accordingly, there are different preferred values for prolonging the *s*, depending on the age and size of the speaker.

   - *Children ages 7 through 10* should be able to sustain an *s* for 8 seconds.
   - *Children ages 11 through 15* should be able to prolong an *s* for 12 seconds.
   - *Women 16 and older* should be able to sustain an *s* for 15 seconds.

- *Men 16 and older* should be able to prolong an *s* for at least 20 seconds.

If you cannot achieve these times, and do not have a respiratory disease, you may want to practice breath control.

2. Counting as far as you can. Different people count at different rates of speed, so for purposes of this test we will measure the number of seconds you can keep counting on one outgoing breath. The more words you say, the more breath you will require, so try to count at a moderate rate.

- *Children under 10 years old* should be able to keep counting for 6 seconds on one breath.
- *Children ages 10 through 15* should be able to count for 8 seconds.
- *Women 16 and older* should be able to count continuously for 10 seconds.
- *Men 16 and older* should be able to count continuously for 12 seconds.

If you cannot achieve these times, you may need practice breath control.

Remember, The Breath Control Test is only a rough screening of how adequate your breath control is. After reading this far in the chapter, you probably already know whether or not you have a breath control problem. If you do, you will want to try some of the suggestions for breath control that follow.

The Breath Control Program

For the typical person with a voice problem, formal teaching of breathing (such as diaphragmatic-abdominal breathing) is usually not necessary. Rather, using simple breath control may be what is most helpful.

The five steps presented here are designed to help you rediscover the breath control that you were born with. One way we will do this is to try to extend your outer limits of breath control. Once you have learned to do that, you can comfortably cut back from those limits so that you always have ample breath for a good, natural voice with minimum effort.

Breathing as a Continuous Motion

As your chest becomes bigger by active muscle action, the air comes in (inspiration). As the chest gets smaller, primarily from muscle relaxation, the air goes out (expiration). From the point of view of producing voice, however, it is important not to view inspiration and expiration as distinctively different events. Ideally, they are one continuous motion.

Two simple exercises in coordinating breathing with walking and talking will help you get a feel for inspiration and expiration as one continuous motion.

1. Take in a breath slowly as you walk five steps. As your leg swings into the sixth step, begin humming for the next five steps. Now keep walking, breathing in again slowly for five steps, and then humming for the next five steps, and so on. Your first five steps are for breathing in, followed by the next five steps breathing out with the voicing of a hum. Practice until this comes easily for you.

2. Take in a breath slowly as you walk five steps. As your leg swings into the sixth step, begin counting one number for each step. Now repeat the cycle, inhaling slowly for five steps, followed by counting 1 through 5 for the next five steps. Keep practicing until this comes easily for you.

Improving Your Expiratory Control

Now that you have developed a feel for inspiration and expiration as one continuous motion, you may also need some practice in prolonging expiration.

In the real world of talking, inspiration is very quick, perhaps about a second long, whereas expiration-talking may last for several seconds. Your results in The Breath Control Test have shown you whether your expiration is adequate for your age and sex. If it is not, the following exercises will help you improve it. As you do them, avoid taking in "the big breath," and don't raise your shoulders or push down. Just take in an easy breath and begin.

1. Using a stopwatch, or a watch or clock with a second hand, see how many seconds on one breath you can prolong (or continue) each of these sounds.

   SSSSS   ZZZZZZ   EEEEEE   AAAAH

   The SSSSS gives us a measure of breath control without voice. The other three sounds are produced with the outgoing airflow creating voice.

2. Use the number of seconds as your baseline measure. If, for example, you can prolong the EEEEE for 8 seconds, 8 seconds is your baseline.
3. Now try prolonging the sounds past your baselines. With practice, you can exceed your baselines by perhaps several seconds. Keep practicing until you can prolong the sounds for about the time limits listed before for your age and sex. Once you know your overall baseline for prolonging these vowel sounds, this can help us find a baseline for how many words we can say on one breath.

Cut Down the Number of Words You Say on One Breath

After hearing a number of voice patients over time, saying too many words on one breath is a common finding. A normal voice requires good breath support. If we have detected some compromise in how long we can prolong a vowel on one breath, a similar timing measure is needed to see how many words we can say on one breath.

Sit or stand tall and see how many words you can say on one breath. To do this, read aloud a simple reading passage or count aloud numbers until you run out of breath. Repeat this procedure maybe three times. Take the highest number as your baseline for number of words on one breath. To be sure you always have enough breath to support what you want to say, try taking your baseline and dividing it by two. For example, if you counted to 16, divide it by two, and you probably would have the best voice without strain if you limited the number of words you say to eight.

This voice clinician (DRB) gives a number of lectures and talks, and I always limit the number of words I say on one breath to eight or nine. My words per breath baseline is around 18. I renew my breath simply by pausing. By cutting that baseline number in half, I experience a more resonant voice without strain. President Barack Obama, during his years as president, gave press conferences and speeches with a clear voice, but usually limiting the number of words he said on one breath to five or six. He would then use a quick pause to renew his breath before continuing to speak.

Give yourself a shortcut to a better voice by cutting down the number of words you say on one breath, pausing, then continue to speak.

Matching Target Models

The average speaker is able to time with amazing accuracy the right amount of breath for what he or she wants to say. For most of us, this process is automatic. We have enough breath, and we have it with no special effort, no audible gasps or body contortions or observable strain. One of the best ways to achieve this easy, natural breathing is by practicing on target model sentences. For example, have someone say a seven-word sentence, such as:

MANY OLD PEOPLE STAYED IN THE KITCHEN.

You will need a partner to help you with this exercise. The partner reads the sentence aloud. You listen. Then the partner points to you to repeat it. Ask the partner to vary the time between when he reads the sentence and when he points at you to repeat it. The idea is for you to repeat the sentence as soon as possible, with no thought about taking in a breath. When you get the cue, say the sentence quickly and in an easy, relaxed manner on one breath. You will be surprised that you usually take in the right amount of air for what you want to say.

Here are some short sentences for you to practice on:

HOW ARE YOU?

HELLO, HOW ARE YOU?

OPEN THE BROWN DOOR.

MONEY, MONEY, LOTS OF MONEY.

AN OLD WOMAN OWNED THE NEW LAND.

HE WENT TO HIS HOME ON THE RANGE.

HAND OVER THE FOUR MISSING ORANGES.

THE YOUNG MAN IN THE CHAIR READ THE PAPER.

SHE WENT OFF HER DIET WHEN SHE DINED OUT.

THE WOMEN IN THE OFFICE TOOK OVER THE COMPANY.

Once you can repeat the target model sentence on cue, without any special breathing effort, practice reading aloud at your own pace, without any signal, using any reading material you wish.

On the Breath Control Test, how many seconds were you able to count on one expiration? Repeating sentences on cue or oral reading on one breath may take only a fraction of that time. The most air most adults would ever need while speaking should be used in less than five seconds.

After a few weeks of practicing matching target models, you will find that you can say more words per breath with very little effort. You will also learn how many words you can comfortably say on one breath. With that information as part of your speaking behavior, you are now ready to learn to pause.

Renewing Breath by Learning to Pause

The magic word for breath control while speaking is pause. It is that simple. So many of us work so hard to breathe while we speak, when all we have to do is pause to renew our breath. When we pause the muscles for inspiration contract, our chest gets bigger, we draw in needed breath, and as we let out the air, we can continue talking comfortably. The pause should become part of your continuous motion of breathing, a reflexive part, one that you are not even aware of. The timing of the pause should not compete with the verbal message. It doesn't need to if we practice finding the right places to pause. Many of our primary school teachers taught us to write in complete sentences, and urged us to speak in complete sentences, too. But that does not mean one complete sentence on each breath. Many sentences are too long for that.

Any place in an utterance that contains natural punctuation, such as a period, semicolon, or comma, is a good place to pause. A good place to pause is also when you are trying to recall a word or an idea, or when you are thinking of what to say next. A poor place for a pause would be between an adjective and a noun [She's a pretty (PAUSE) girl], or between a verb and an adverb [He ran (PAUSE) fast].

Using any kind of recorder, practice reading the following paragraphs, pausing where indicated in the text.

> HARVEY'S WIFE, *pause* JOANNE, *pause* FOUND OUT ONE DAY THAT SHE WAS ACTUALLY HARVEY'S FIFTH WIFE, *pause* THAT HE HAD A SERIES OF MARRIAGES *pause* ONE RIGHT AFTER THE OTHER. *pause* EACH OF THE NEW WIVES HAD NO KNOWLEDGE *pause* THAT HARVEY WAS ALREADY MARRIED, *pause* AND CERTAINLY NOT *pause* "SEVERAL TIMES BEFORE." *pause* BY TALKING WITH OTHER WOMEN AT HER HEALTH CLUB, *pause* JOANNE FOUND OUT THE NAMES AND ADDRESSES OF THE OTHER WIVES *pause* TO WHOM HARVEY WAS STILL MARRIED. *pause* JOANNE GATHERED ALL OF THE WIVES TOGETHER ONE NIGHT. *pause* EACH WOMAN THOUGHT THAT HARVEY WAS A TRAVELING SALESMAN, *pause* WHICH WAS WHY HE ONLY CAME *pause* "HOME" ONCE A WEEK. *pause* TOGETHER, pause THEY PLANNED A HOMECOMING THAT HARVEY WOULD NEVER FORGET.

Sometimes the pause before a word or phrase gives special meaning to what is being said:

> IN THE NEW AGE OF SCIENCE AND SPACE, *pause* IMPROVED EDUCATION IS ESSENTIAL TO GIVE NEW

MEANING *pause* TO OUR NATIONAL PURPOSE AND POWER. *pause* IN THE LAST 20 YEARS, *pause* MANKIND HAS ACQUIRED MORE SCIENTIFIC INFORMATION *pause* THAN IN ALL OF PREVIOUS HISTORY. *pause* NINETY PERCENT OF ALL THE SCIENTISTS THAT EVER LIVED *pause* ARE ALIVE AND WORKING TODAY. *pause* VAST STRETCHES OF THE UNKNOWN ARE BEING EXPLORED EVERY DAY. *pause* FOR MILITARY, MEDICAL, COMMER-CIAL, *pause* AND OTHER REASONS. *pause* FINALLY, *pause* THE TWISTING COURSE OF THE COLD WAR *pause* REQUIRES A CITIZENRY THAT UNDERSTAND OUR PRIN-CIPLES AND PROBLEMS. *pause* IT REQUIRES SKILLED MANPOWER *pause* AND BRAINPOWER *Pause* TO MATCH THE POWER OF TOTALITARIAN DISCIPLINE. *pause* IT REQUIRES A SCIENTIFIC EFFORT, *pause* WHICH DEMON-STRATES THE SUPERIORITY OF FREEDOM. *pause* AND IT REQUIRES AN ELECTORATE IN EVERY STATE *pause* WITH SUFFICIENTLY BROAD HORIZONS AND SUFFI-CIENT MATURITY AND JUDGMENT *pause* TO GUIDE THIS NATION SAFELY THROUGH WHATEVER LIES AHEAD.[1]

The commas, periods, and stress places in the above paragraphs provide natural places to pause. During each pause, your breath should have been renewed naturally, with no special effort on your part.

Now listen to the playback recording of your reading. Are those natural places for you to pause? Do you need to pause more often or less often? Try pausing in different places in the text than the ones I marked. Now listen to how the pauses work for your breath control, and for the sense of the material. You may want to ask someone else to listen to your recording and see how they evaluate you for ease of speaking and for the sense of what you are saying.

Practice with paragraphs from books and magazines. Mark them for pauses. Then read paragraphs you haven't marked to see if you are developing a natural feel for when you need to pause.

---

[1]Excerpted from a speech to the U.S. Congress by President John F. Kennedy, January 29, 1963.

Pausing easily transfers to the real world of talking. One of the first things you will find out is that your listeners don't run away when you pause. In fact, if anything, the pause will make you a more effective speaker. Good pauses make your meaning clearer. Good pauses give a natural emphasis to those parts of what you are saying that you want to stress. And the pause, so brief that it is hardly noticeable, gives you the continuous breath supply you need for speech.

Too little air, too many words, too much effort. Any of these symptoms while speaking are clear signs that you may not be allowing your natural breathing to function. Because breathing for speech can become as automatic as your heartbeat or blinking, correcting your problem is not a matter of learning something difficult and new. By following the suggestions in this Breath Control Program, you will do what you were born knowing how to do: breathe easily enough to speak in a normal, natural voice.

CHAPTER 6

Loud Enough or Too Loud?

"Your voice has a loudness control, too."

Your Loudness Control

Radio, television, and smartphones have a loudness control. We can adjust their volume to a comfortable level so that music or speech is intelligible, yet not so loud or so faint that it is annoying. When it comes to our voices, however, many of us fail to realize that we need to use a loudness control in just as discriminating a manner. We need to adjust the loudness of our voices for different speaking situations.

An overly loud voice can signal that the speaker is aggressive and unfriendly, brash, boorish, or insensitive. Or such a loud voice may be spoken by someone with a severe hearing loss. A voice that is too soft can suggest that the speaker is shy, indecisive, has low self-esteem, or doesn't really care to communicate. Or perhaps the excessively soft voice is spoken by someone who does not feel well.

Like other voice characteristics discussed in this book, the loudness of your voice may be telling on you, and it may tell the wrong story. Loudness conveys the strength of our feelings, our level of confidence, and whether we are anxious or hostile or comfortable with those around us. We use loudness to project our voices across distance, yet our loudness level also conveys the emotional distance we want with other people. A voice that is too loud keeps people at length. A voice that is too soft can signal that you don't want to bridge the gap between other people and yourself.

We need to vary our level of loudness for physical distances between us and our listeners, to accommodate for different levels of background noise, and to convey different emotions (which we may or may not wish to show). The problem is that many people use the same level of loudness all the time. They may do this for a variety of reasons.

Take the case of Ed, the 55-year-old Dean of a School of Business Administration at a major university. Visitors to his office were quickly turned off by a voice so loud that he seemed aggressive. As one colleague put it, "He's always giving a speech instead of just talking with you."

In fact, as part of his work, Ed did give a lot of speeches to business groups. And, over the years, he had begun to emulate the speaking style of the hard-charging executives and entrepreneurs he had met and admired.

Although such a voice might have been appropriate for his lecture audiences, students and faculty reacted differently. His colleagues thought him authoritarian and a man who liked to talk more than listen. Students were so intimidated by him that they dreaded visits to his office, and often came away not remembering what he said.

When Ed finally came to us, we heard at once that the voice he used in our offices was not the voice that was giving him his problem. What we heard was the moderate voice of a man who had realized that he had a voice problem and wanted to do something about it.

Which was Ed's real voice, the one that caused his colleagues to refer to him (he learned only recently) as "Thundering Ed," or the softer voice of the man who came to us for help? It was both. Ed hadn't realized that the loudness level appropriate for one speaking situation and one kind of audience might not be appropriate elsewhere, in fact, most of the people he spoke with weren't an "audience" at all.

Ed confessed to us that he had come to like his hard-charging voice. He liked the image of himself that he thought it projected.

Without giving it much more thought than that, he had adopted it as his customary voice.

We were able to show him exercises to help him find his volume control, so that he could adapt his loudness for different settings, yet still command attention and carry conviction. "Thundering Ed" still inspires them on the lecture circuit, but colleagues, students, and friends are far more comfortable with his "voice of moderation."

Like Ed, all of us can learn to use some volume control for our voices. Relatively early in life, most of us learned to use the loudness level that got things done for us, that produced the reaction we wanted. For example, when we are with a loved one we use a softer voice. When we want the kids to turn down their stereo, we often find that a loud voice is necessary. In some business or professional situations, we may need to speak a little more loudly to add authority to our voices. But some people either are uncertain what volume level is appropriate, or for other reasons, fall back on using the same level of volume in most situations. Habitual loudness levels can cause problems.

That was the case with Samantha, a 28-year-old secretary. Being a secretary was not her choice of career. She had studied to be a teacher and even had her teaching credential. But in her student-teaching days she discovered that her voice was not loud enough for students sitting back in the classroom to hear, unless she really "forced" her voice. When she did, her voice would not last through the day. She would be physically exhausted, and her throat felt raw.

Instead of trying to change her voice ("I didn't know I could, I thought it was something I was born with," she told us), Samantha decided to change careers. However, the problem that had plagued her in the classroom followed her to the large medical office where she worked as a secretary. Although she could be understood better on the telephone, like many soft-spoken people can, Samantha had problems being understood by the team of doctors she worked with and by some of their patients. She was always being asked to "speak up," or to repeat things she had said.

When Samantha came to us for help, we discovered that the voice she was "born with" was in fact a voice that she had acquired because it seemed to please other people. Hers was a little-girl voice, one that early in her life her parents and friends had found cute. Later, her dates in high school and college not only found it cute, but sexy. Samantha's voice was light and breathy and had so little volume that people had to lean closer to hear what she was saying.

A voice evaluation showed that Samantha's breath inhalation for talking was no greater than what she used just sitting in front of her laptop. As a result, besides speaking almost inaudibly at times, she commonly ran out of breath when she spoke, leaving some of her sentences incomplete. Listeners not only had trouble understanding her, they thought she didn't have much to say or, at any rate, didn't care to communicate it.

We were able to help Samantha, first of all, by showing her that her "cute" voice was not her natural voice, but a very artificial one. Once she realized that, we were able to show her techniques, which were described in the last chapter, for taking in larger breaths and pausing more often when she spoke. With a more available air supply, she could speak louder without strain. With adequate pauses in her speech, she could renew her breath and complete all of her sentences with plenty of needed volume.

Samantha discovered that speaking loudly enough to be easily understood made her much more effective and appreciated in her work. Also, it was far from a drawback socially. She found that now people paid attention to her for what she said and not for the ineffective way she once said it.

Appropriate Loudness

In noisy environments, most of us adjust our loudness level automatically. At a rock concert, on a jet plane, or talking to someone using a power mower, we raise our voice loudness until we can be heard. In contrast, in a church, a hospital, or near a room where someone is sleeping, we lower our voice volume so it is not disturbing.

The noise levels in our immediate environment are very obvious clues to the loudness levels we need to use. Many people, like Ed and Samantha, had trouble adjusting loudness in more ordinary circumstances. Ed would not dream of dressing inappropriately for a lecture, nor Samantha for her day at the office. But neither had exercised the same sensitivity for their voices.

To help you gain awareness of how loudly you customarily speak, we have developed a Loudness Rating Scale. For each loudness level, we have listed the average intensity level measured on a sound level meter. Fortunately, there are many APPS available today for your use for measuring the intensity (loudness) of your voice on a decibel (dB) scale. For example, while speaking or reading aloud on your smartphone or tablet, the loudness app will give you digital feedback as to the voice intensity you are using. We have labeled five loudness levels on our Loudness Rating Scale:

1. **Whisper** (30 dB). We use no voice at all as we whisper to someone near us.
2. **Soft Voice** (35–50 dB). The kind of voice that would not awaken someone sleeping nearby.
3. **Conversational Voice** (55–75 dB). This is a loudness level that usually matches that of the people with whom we are speaking.
4. **Loud Voice** (80–90 dB). This is the voice we use in front of a group (without using a microphone), or when we want to command attention.
5. **Yelling** (100+ dB). We use this when we are angry, or demand to be heard, or in sports, as players or spectators.

Keep these loudness ratings in mind as you take the simple test that follows. It will give you a clearer idea of the relative loudness of your voice and is the first step for gaining control of any changes needed in your voice loudness.

The Voice Loudness Test

By following these three test steps, you can tell whether or not you need to alter your customary loudness. The latter part of this chapter will give you exercises for changing and controlling your level of loudness.

1. Gather around a table with a few friends or colleagues will-ing to help you with the test. (They might find the results interesting for their own voices.) In the center of the table place a recorder, and record five minutes or so of spontane-ous discussion in which you each actively participate. Now listen to the playback.

   • Is the loudness of your voice similar to that of the other participants? If it is, your loudness in this situation seems adequate; on the Loudness Rating Scale, your voice would probably be a Level 3, conversational voice.
   • If the loudness of your voice is different from that of the others, would you rate yourself as a Level 2 (soft voice) or a Level 4 (loud voice)? We assume that you neither whis-pered nor yelled. If you were consistently louder than the others, you need to learn to soften your voice. If you were consistently softer, you need to increase your loudness.

   Both kinds of exercises will be given later. But first complete the other two steps.

2. Find a voice loudness app on your smartphone that can provide you with an average of your voice intensity taken while reading aloud for two or three minutes. Where does your average dB level place you on the Loudness Rating Scale? An average level below 55 dB may indicate the need to increase your loudness. Values in excess of 80 dB indicate you may be talking too loudly.

3. This step will help you think about your own voice loudness. Do you really need to change your voice loudness? As accu-rately as you can, respond true or false to these statements below about your voice.

   • I vary the loudness of my voice as I speak.
   • My voice loudness is appropriate for most speaking situations.
   • People seldom ask me to repeat what I have said.
   • People seldom ask me to speak more softly.
   • People seldom ask me to speak louder.
   • Overall, I am pleased with my voice loudness.

   If you answered true to each statement, your voice loudness is probably adequate, although you may want to check your rating with that of some of your friends. If one or more of the statements seem to apply to you, you probably need to work on your voice loudness level.

What we are concerned with is a customary level of loudness that is inappropriately loud or soft. If the above tests suggest that you need to decrease or increase your level of loudness, the exercises that follow will be of help.

Exercises for Changing Your Voice Loudness

Decreasing Voice Loudness

First of all, it is important to realize that a common cause of an overly loud voice is hearing loss. Hard-of-hearing speakers generally use a louder voice, and are often slow to realize that they have a hearing problem. If there is any question of hearing loss, have your hearing checked by an audiologist or otolaryngologist (ear-nose-throat doctor). Correcting a hearing loss would have to be the first step in altering one's voice loudness.

If hearing loss is not the cause of your speaking too loudly, the first step in correcting the problem is to become aware that the problem exists. The Voice Loudness Test has helped you do this. Now, a little practice with the following exercises can help you to develop a softer voice.

1. Review the five loudness levels in the Loudness Rating Scale (whisper, soft voice, conversational voice, loud voice, and yelling). See if you can produce these levels in various sequences. We will omit practice in yelling because it is hard on the larynx and the ears of anyone listening to you. Try saying HELLO, HOW ARE YOU? at four loudness levels, varying the order in which they occur, as illustrated below.

   • soft–loud–whisper–conversation
   • loud–whisper–conversation–soft
   • whisper–soft–conversation–loud
   • conversation–whisper–loud–soft
   • soft–conversation–whisper–loud

Now try counting to ten using the different loudness levels as above. To fix the differences clearly in your mind, it may be helpful for you look at your intensity levels measured by your apps and displayed on your screen. You will soon realize that the loud voice level requires a lot more effort. It is easier to use the whisper or soft voice. This exercise helps you develop your own "loudness control" so that, as you do with your radio, television, or phone, you can adjust your speech volume so that it is intelligible and comfortable for you and your listeners.

2. Now that you can produce different loudness levels, try using the soft voice level in some conversational situations. You may be surprised how often it is an appropriate voice, even though most of the time outside your home Level 3 (conversational voice) is what you want to use. Level 4 (loud voice) should only be used in situations when increased volume is necessary for others to hear you, such as in noisy environments or before large groups when there is no amplification. What you are developing with this exercise is sensitivity to the appropriate loudness level for different speaking situations. The best rule is: never use a loudness level greater than necessary.

3. Also, develop your sensitivity to the varying noise levels around you, at home, in your car, at work, and in recreational settings. Before you speak, take a second to register the noise level in your immediate environment. After you have done this for awhile, you will automatically adjust your voice loudness level so that you can always be heard above the background noise.

Increasing Voice Loudness

We need to devote a little more space to these exercises than the previous one because speaking too softly seems to be a more common problem than speaking too loudly. This is particularly the case among women because so many of them have been conditioned to think that a soft voice is more feminine, or, unfortunately, conditioned to not be assertive.

Once the Voice Loudness Test has made you aware that you need to speak louder in certain situations, the following practice steps will help you use a louder voice.

1. Develop your sensitivity to situations where others have trouble understanding you. Where do you most often hear reactions such as, "Would you please say that again?" These are obvious clues that you need to speak louder. But there are less obvious clues too, in facial expressions and body language. If listeners look bored, inattentive, or fidget when you talk, it may not be because of what you are saying, but how you are saying it. Nothing tries people's patience more than a speaker who does not make himself be heard. A speaker who is too loud may irritate, or even affront some listeners, but one who speaks too softly can forfeit his listener's attention completely.

2. Determine if the background noise (such as from a CD player or machinery noise) can be reduced. If you can reduce the noise level around you, this would be an obvious first step for improving how others can hear you. Do not proceed to steps 3 to 11 until you have done what you can do to reduce the loudness levels around you.

3. Check your articulation. Are you a mumbler? Some people habitually fail to articulate sounds such as *t*, *d*, *sh*, *ch*, *k*, *g*, *f*, and *v*. Articulation and loudness usually go hand in hand. If you do not articulate clearly, no amount of volume will help you be understood. On the other hand, articulated speech at too low a volume is still indistinct speech. Listen to a recording of your own speech. Do you make the sounds listed above as clearly as they can be made? If this is particularly difficult for you, you might want to consult a speech-language pathologist (see Chapter 16) for some help in articulation improvement.

4. An easy way to make your voice louder is to take in a slightly larger than normal breath. As you probably discovered in experimenting with the levels of the Loudness Rating Scale, speaking louder not only requires more effort, it takes more air. Try it. Try saying, "HELLO, HOW ARE YOU?" taking in varying amounts of air before you speak. Practice this until

you automatically take in the right amount of air for the loudness you want.

5. One way to be sure you have enough air for an adequate loudness level is to cut down on the total number of words you say on one breath. Using a recorder, check the number of words you customarily say on a breath. If lack of air causes your voice to become softer, cut the number of words you say on one breath; for example, if you say 15 words, cut the number on one breath down to 10. In other words, pause more often. Use your recorder and check the apps for loudness levels while experimenting until you find the number of words between pauses that consistently gives you adequate voice volume.

6. Elevating your voice pitch by about one note can also make your voice easier to hear. Level 2 (soft voice) can often sound like Level 3 (conversational voice) when you raise your pitch a note. In Chapter 7 we will show you ways to elevate your voice pitch. For many of you who have problems being heard in conversational or work situations, raising your pitch level may be all you need to do.

7. Practice reading aloud, combining what we have just said about pausing more often and elevating your pitch level a note. Record your reading. First, read with your old, customary voice. Then use the breathing and pitch elevation tips for the second reading. Listen to the playback. Check your loudness on you intensity app. You should sound louder. If you do not, steps 10, and 11, which follow, should help you.

8. There is also a lifting technique that you can practice to produce a louder voice. Once you experience producing this louder voice, you will no longer need to use the lifting exercise. Here is how it works:

   • Sit in a chair with your arms extended below the seat on each side. Count aloud 1 to 10. As you count, reach under the seat and try to lift the chair off the floor. You won't be able to get the chair off the floor, of course, but the muscular exertion used should increase your breath force, increasing the strength of your vocal fold vibration, and result in a louder voice.

- Repeat the counting and lifting action while recording the exercise. On playback, can you hear a louder voice while trying to lift? If you did, go back and practice exercises 3, 4, and 5. Now that you have found a louder voice, these exercises will help you control it when you want to.

9. By now, you probably can produce a louder voice more often. See if you can sustain this louder voice while reading aloud. You can get some feedback as to how well you are able to speak louder by finding an app that looks at how well you can produce a louder voice at a fixed loudness level. Set a voice intensity level, below which you will receive an auditory or visual wrong alarm. For example, if you set the lowest level at 50 dB and your voice drops to 49 dB or lower, you will hear or see the feedback indicating you need to increase your voice loudness. This oral reading practice has been found often to be most valuable for helping to increase the loudness of one's voice.

10. Open your mouth a bit more when you speak. Many people who mumble or speak too softly do so because they do not open their mouths enough when they speak. This may be a problem of yours.

    - Look at yourself in a mirror or video playback as you speak. Do you open your mouth, or do you speak through clenched teeth and closed lips?
    - Try opening your mouth more when you speak. Allow your lips to shape the words and syllables. You would be unable to speak distinctly if someone put his hand over your mouth when you tried to talk. Keeping your mouth closed is like putting a hand over your own mouth.

11. This step will require someone else to help you. You will also need to wear earphones connected to some kind of music source such as on your iPod or tablet, a radio, or a stereo.

    - Put on your earphones and listen to some kind of music at low intensity levels.
    - Instruct the other person to increase suddenly the volume of the music as you are reading aloud into a recorder.
    - After reading aloud for two or three minutes, stop and listen to the playback. You will be amazed at how loud

and clear your voice can sound when you speak with loud music in your ears.

- Once you have recorded and saved your louder voice, you can use it as a model for practice, just as you did with the lifting exercise. Your memory of your louder voice will be good enough so that you usually will be able to match it without needing the loud noise or music in the background. Reinforce your control by going back and practicing exercises 3, 4, and 5.

If, after all of the above, you still have a problem making a louder voice, turn to Chapter 8. Is Your Voice in Focus? In that chapter we talk about bringing the focus of your voice out of your throat and placing it in the general area of the mouth. A well-focused voice, coming from the front of the mouth, usually produces a louder voice.

Now that you have learned how to adjust and use the "loudness control" of your voice in various situations, you should find that you can always speak at a loudness level where you can be heard and understood—but never louder than necessary. An appropriate level of loudness is one of the keys to your natural voice.

CHAPTER 7

The Well-Aimed Pitch

*"You can really throw your listeners a curve
with an inappropriately pitched voice."*

Pitch is a key element of our voice "fingerprint," one of the characteristics that makes our voices distinctively our own. Even without seeing a person, voice pitch helps tell us immediately whether the speaker is male or female, and roughly what his or her age may be.

From pitch, we can gather other information, too. Although there are normal pitch ranges for each sex and age group, there is considerable variation in habitual pitch level individual to individual. Moreover, when we speak, most of us vary our pitch in a distinctive manner, stressing some words and not others. (We do this with loudness, too.) This pattern of rising and falling pitches we call voice inflection.

Both our habitual pitch level and our pattern of inflection help pinpoint who we are and what kind of person we are. We often reveal our emotions by changes in our pitch and pitch inflections. For example, fear can often be heard by higher pitch and rising inflection; anger can be heard in lower pitch and downward pitch inflections (usually coupled with greater voice loudness). As is true with other elements of voice, often we have acquired these pitch characteristics sometime in our past and have taken them for granted as part of our voice. But a voice that is pitched too high can make an otherwise masculine man sound feminine. A woman's voice that is pitched too high can make her sound like a person who is not to be taken seriously. For either sex, a voice pitched lower than it should be can strain the vocal equipment and lower one's speech intelligibility. And all of us know how tiring and irritating a monotonous voice without inflections can be. In short, a mispitched voice can send an inaccurate or unfavorable message about us and may damage our vocal folds.

This was the case with Sammy, 25 years old and a new biology teacher at a suburban high school. He felt he looked too young for his age, and that because he did, he had discipline problems with his classes and was not as effective a teacher as he knew he could be. Sammy's reaction was to do a number of things to seem older, like wearing dark, conservative suits and discarding his contact lenses in favor of glasses, and stopping shaving to grow facial hair.

He also tried speaking in as low a voice as he could to sound more mature. The result of this, however, was hoarseness and sometimes loss of voice toward the end of the school day. The problem became so severe that eventually he came to our voice clinic.

Pitch or frequency testing at our clinic found his lowest note to be an A2 (110 Hz) and his highest note near a D4 (274 Hz), giving him a vocal range of about eleven full musical notes. Unfortunately, his most frequent note while talking in the clinic was a B2, just a note above the lowest note he could produce. We found that he was speaking most of the time at the bottom of his pitch range. We advised him to raise his regular speaking pitch up two or three notes. (Most of us use a pitch two to three notes above our lowest note.) We gave him practice exercises to do this, and within two weeks his hoarseness had disappeared.

We will soon show you how to find your own natural pitch level, and how to raise and lower your pitch, if you need to do so. The point about Sammy is that his voice strain was caused by constantly speaking below his natural pitch level.

Some people have the opposite problem: speaking above their natural pitch level. This is sometimes found among girls or women who imagine that a higher pitch will make them sound more feminine. But if this is not the natural pitch for their voices, the result can be the same voice strain that Sammy experienced.

No one should speak at the same pitch level all of the time. Rather, pitch will usually vary with inflections up and down. However, there does appear to be one pitch level that we hear most of the time in a speaking voice, which we identify as the person's habitual pitch. When the habitual pitch is near the natural pitch, we generally have a healthy voice. What we call a natural pitch level is when the voice is produced with the least amount of muscular effort. This easy voice can usually be heard in the easily produced voice we use in agreeing with another person over what he or she has just said, saying "uhm huh." We call this natural voice the "voice of agreement."

We usually find the natural pitch several notes above the bottom of our pitch range. The natural pitch often includes more than one note, sometimes adding the note above it or the note below it. The human voice does not cling to one speaking note. Although we can identify one habitual pitch in the voice, it is important to remember that there is continuous fluctuation above and below this pitch.

Let us look first at what the natural pitch levels are for children, men, and women of various age groups. Then we will give you some simple tasks to find whether your habitual speaking pitch is approximately where it should be and give you exercises to raise or lower it, if it is not. Finally, we will make some recommendations for gaining control of pitch so that your speech has good pitch inflection.

Finding Your Pitch Level

In our voice clinics we have electronic instruments that quickly tell us what pitch level a person is using. There are, also, many apps available, such as "Measuring Voice Pitch," that can measure pitch range and habitual pitch (one's most used pitch level). The frequency of vibration per second is known as the hertz (Hz) value. The Hz value can also be expressed in the notes of the musical scale as played on a conventional 88-key piano. Fortunately for us as we work on pitch, there are now [post-2015] a number of apps that measure hertz values and musical note designations. This can give us pitch feedback on the various pitch tasks and exercises we will be using later in this chapter. Although many of you will not have access to a piano, for purposes of illustration, we show in Figure 7–1, Piano Keyboard, where the natural pitches of the voice fall in terms of musical notes.

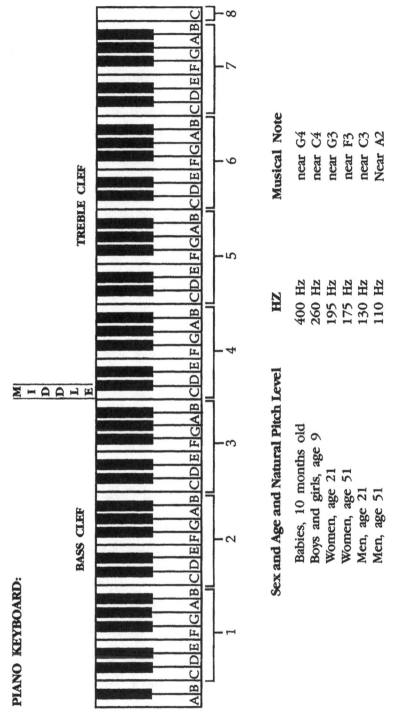

Figure 7-1. Typical speaking pitch levels for age and sex.

You will notice that the keyboard is divided into octaves with each full octave consisting of the notes (the piano white keys) C-D-E-F-G-A-B. The black keys represent the flats and sharps between the white keys. The lowest note on the keyboard is A1, the highest is C8, and middle C midway on the keyboard is called C4. The number designation coupled to the musical note is where that note occurs (left toward right) in which octave on the musical keyboard; for example, C3 is lower by an octave than C4.

In Figure 7–1, we show the typical pitch levels for certain ages and sex. The pitch levels shown are normal, natural pitch levels, the kind of pitch we often use when we agree with someone by using the "voice of agreement" when we say "uhm huh." As you can see, the speaking voice pitches of adult men and women fall only in the range of octaves 2, 3, and 4.

Both the normal pitch level and overall pitch range (from the lowest to the highest note you can reach) can vary individual to individual. Some of us have naturally lower or higher pitched voices than others.

The basic pitch level and range of the voice is determined by the physical size of the larynx. But we ourselves change our voice pitch as we speak, or sing, by changing the tension of the vocal folds. When they are contracted and thick, we produce lower pitches. When they are stretched, the tension on the folds increases and we produce higher pitches. In normal conversation at our natural pitch level, the vocal folds need very little stretching. Consequently, our voice sounds relaxed and resonant. This is the goal we need to achieve.

Two Self-Tests for Finding Your Natural Pitch Level

There are two ways we can find out what our natural pitch level should be. A simple way that requires no musical knowledge is our first self-test, The "Uhm Huh" Voice Pitch Test. Our second pitch test, the Music-Assisted Voice Pitch Test, requires some basic musical knowledge. We usually find that the "uhm huh" and the music-assisted tests identify the same natural pitch level, but the music-assisted test identifies the pitch more precisely by musical note.

The "Uhm Huh" Voice Pitch Test

You may or may not be using a natural pitch level. One way to find out is to take this simple test.

1. Use your smartphone or a recorder. Read aloud a paragraph from the newspaper and record it. Listen closely to the pitch of your voice on playback. Does your pitch level sound too high or too low? Does your pitch seem to vary up and down as it should?
2. Make a recording of conversation with several of your friends (all of the same sex). Listen to the playback. Does your voice pitch sound similar to the voices of the other men or women? If your pitch sounds lower or higher, you may have some realistic concern of your voice pitch level.
3. Record yourself when saying "uhm huh." It is best to do this by reading a question aloud before saying it. Read the question and then stop. And then say "uhm huh" as if you were responding to a question. For example, read aloud

   DO YOU BELIEVE THAT THE AMERICAN PUBLIC WANTS SPACE EXPLORATION?

   Now answer, "uhm huh." Repeat this several times.
4. More often than not, the "uhm huh" has been said at a pitch that is very near your natural pitch. Listen to the pitch level of your "uhm huh" several times. See if you can match it by saying "one, one, one" at the same pitch level. Listen to your playback. Does your saying "one, one, one" show a pitch level that you feel needs to be higher or lower in pitch? How does it vary from the pitch you used in saying "uhm huh" and when reading the sentence out loud?
5. Say other questions aloud, and follow each by answering "uhm huh." Listen carefully to the playback. If you feel that

your pitch level and your pitch inflection are not problems for you, you can skip reading the balance of this chapter.

If you feel you want to raise or lower your habitual pitch after your experience with the "uhm huh" testing, you might turn to the "Uhm Huh" Pitch Practice exercises given later in this chapter. If you want to work now on pitch variability, go to Practice in Varying Your Pitch.

The Music-Assisted Voice Pitch Test

For the reader who has a good musical ear and access to some kind of instrument (piano, guitar, pitch app), this self-test is much more precise in determining habitual and natural pitch levels than the "uhm huh" self-test.

This test requires an app, or a recorder, or an instrument that can produce a single note. Your task will be to play a note, or have someone else play it, and see if you can vocally match it. If you have a good ear, you can do the test by yourself. If you have difficulty finding the notes or matching the pitches with your voice, ask someone to help you.

1. Select a note easily produced by persons your age and sex. Play this note (see keyboard in Figure 7–1) as your model:
   - Teenage girls, play G3
   - Teenage boys, play D3
   - Adult women, play F3
   - Adult men, play B2

2. Some people can more easily match their voice pitch to another voice than to the note of an instrument (like a piano or harmonica). Some people cannot produce an isolated pitch that is supposed to match an external instrument model. If this is a problem for you, ask a friend of the same age-gender as you to voice the note for you. Use their voice pitch as your model. Record their voice model so you can use the model for future practice. If you can easily match a pitch model, go on to steps 3 and beyond.

3. Match the model note by saying "eee" at that same note. Then sing down one note at a time, saying "eee" until you produce the lowest "eee" you can make. For example, if you started at B2, the adult male model note, you would sing down, saying "eee," voicing the notes B2, A2, G2, and F2. Your lowest note would be F2.

4. Our natural pitch levels are usually a few notes above our lowest note. Start with your lowest note and say "eee." Go up one note at a time for just two more notes. This could be very close to your natural pitch level, a note that you can produce with very little effort.

5. Now sing up two notes, saying "eee" above your lowest note. This note, too, could be a natural pitch level for you. Most of us have one or two notes that we produce easily. Remember, the natural pitch level for speaking is always a few notes (two or three) higher than the lowest note you can sing. But, most important, stay off the very bottom of your pitch range when you use your voice.

Now that you know where your natural pitch ought to be, find out what your habitual pitch is. Record some conversational speech and oral reading. Listen carefully to the playback. Introduce your natural pitch level (the pitch you just determined) and compare it with your recording. You might ask someone else to help you make this judgment. Is your habitual pitch at the same level as your natural pitch? If it is, you probably do not have to work on changing pitch.

If you want to change your habitual pitch to more closely match your natural pitch, the exercises that follow will help you.

Practice in Producing Your Natural Speaking Pitch

Learning to relax the vocal tract can help you find your natural pitch and maintain it once you have found it. With less tension, the vocal folds produce the pitch level that is natural for them. Here are two techniques that are helpful for getting this relaxation.

The Yawn-Sigh Method

Taking in a bigger breath on a yawn, and letting it out on a sigh, immediately relaxes the mouth and throat. Practice prolonging sounds as you sigh. First yawn (with no voice) and then sigh out the air with light voice. Your pitch level on the sigh will be close to your natural pitch. Practice extending the sigh using these five sounds:

AAAAAAAH   AAAAAAARM   AAAAAAALL   HAM   HARM

The sigh-induced voice is particularly good practice for those who need to lower their voice pitch.

The Chewing Method

Many people with pitch problems don't open their mouths as wide as they should, and often speak through clenched teeth. This is a tense way to speak. The chewing approach will help develop an open, relaxed mouth and throat. After practice in speaking while chewing, your voice will produce a pitch very near your natural pitch level. This exercise may not be pretty to look at, but it is fun to do and it works.

1. Practice chewing in front of a mirror. Open your mouth at least two fingers wide between your teeth. Move your jaw and tongue up and down and exaggerate the movement of your mouth.
2. Add light voice while you chew. This will produce a monotonous yahm-yahm-yahm kind of sound.
3. Now practice saying these nonsense words as you chew:

   MOONAMONGA   ALAMETERAH   CUCALAMONGA

   Prolong the words as you say them until they sound almost like a chant. The voice you produce while doing this should be near the natural pitch level that you are trying to achieve.

These exercises are useful for reminding yourself what your natural pitch level sounds like and also will help you to relax your mouth and throat so that you can produce it.

We now need to consider some specific exercises for either lowering or raising your pitch level.

Practice in Lowering Your Pitch

On either of the two previous tests, if you found that you need to lower your pitch level, the practice steps below can help you. The first practice session uses the "uhm huh" as your reference voice. The second section uses actual musical pitch as your practice guide.

Using the "Uhm Huh" as Your Practice Guide

1. Use the steps you used in the "uhm huh" test to establish your practice "uhm huh." This "uhm huh" is a lower pitch than you generally use, otherwise you wouldn't be trying to lower your habitual pitch to this new, lower level. As we practice on other words, we will always come back to your "uhm huh" as your reference sound.
2. Record your "uhm huh" several times. Listen to the playback. Can you reproduce it just as it sounds on the recording? If not, practice with your recorder until you can always produce the "uhm huh" the same way. Once you can comfortably produce the "uhm huh," go ahead to the next practice step.
3. Practice saying the "uhm huh" followed immediately by repeating these words:

ONE   ONE   ONE

MAN   MAN   MAN

MANY   MANY   MANY

ONE-TWO-THREE-FOUR-FIVE

ONE-TWO-THREE-FOUR-FIVE-SIX-SEVEN-EIGHT-
NINE-TEN

Record this practice step. Listen to the playback. Does your pitch level on the words stay on the same level as on the "uhm huh"? Repeat it so that all the words are on the same "uhm huh" pitch level.

4. Read aloud from a magazine or newspaper. About every 10 words, say "uhm huh" and try to maintain that kind of pitch level for the total reading. Record your oral reading practice. Did you stay at the lower pitch?

Using a Musical Pitch as Your Practice Guide

1. The easiest way to lower your pitch, if you have a good ear, is to play the note that represents your natural pitch. You can use a piano or a musical note generated by your pitch app. Use this now as your practice note. See if you can match it with your own voice pitch. Prolong the pitch with an extended "ah." Practice reading aloud in a monotone using this new pitch. Make a recording of your voice using the new pitch in both reading and conversation. Keep your voice at a monotone, using the new pitch for all words. Listen to the playback. If you are satisfied that you kept the lower pitch throughout the reading, go on to the next step. If keeping the new pitch is difficult, repeat the first two steps.

2. Speak in your higher voice, the one that you found was your habitual pitch. Take a word like man and prolong saying it at that pitch level for about three seconds. It will sound like *maaaaaan.* Now practice saying *man,* prolonging the length of the word, as you descend down the musical scale to the lowest note you can produce. Record your practice effort as you say:

MAN (your habitual pitch)

    MAN

       MAN***

         MAN

           MAN

Now listen to the playback carefully. Did the words sound better—more resonant, louder, and more relaxed—at one of the pitches? If so, this could well be your natural pitch level. Practice saying the word, two or three notes from the bottom. Was the best sounding word the one that is marked ***? Often, your best, or natural, pitch level is two notes above your lowest note.

3. Keep practicing the lower pitch level until you find it comfortable. It may take a few days of practice.

Practice in Raising Your Pitch

A voice with too low a pitch level usually lacks carrying power, projection, and full resonance. If, on the previous tests, you found that you needed to raise your pitch, some of these suggestions will help you.

Using the "Uhm-Huh" as Your Practice Guide

You found on testing that your habitual pitch was lower than the pitch you use when you say "uhm huh." Use your recorder for these practice suggestions and listen carefully to the playback.

1. Speak at your regular pitch level (the one you found was too low). Read a sentence or two from a newspaper, suddenly stop, and say "uhm huh." Listen to the playback. Is the "uhm huh" slightly higher in pitch? Now read again but try to keep it at the higher "uhm huh" level. If you were able to do this, try to do more reading at the higher level.
2. Go back to your regular, lower voice. Say "one, one, one" at that lower level. Now see if you can go "one, one, one" up the scale from your regular voice, like this:

ONE

ONE

ONE***

ONE

ONE (your low, regular voice)

Listen to the third word (marked ***) closely. This might be the higher pitch you are looking for. See if you can match this higher pitch with other words than "one."
3. Practice saying words in a monotone at the higher pitch level, the one marked ***. Do some monotone reading at the same higher pitch level.

You have now found a higher pitch level, perhaps at or near your natural pitch level. You might now try to practice speaking at this level.

Using a Musical Pitch as Your Practice Guide

1. The easiest way to raise your habitual pitch is to play the note that you tested as your natural pitch on a piano or on a pitch app that can generate musical notes. Attempt to match it with your own voice. Prolong the natural pitch with an extended "ah." Practice reading aloud in a monotone voice with the new pitch. Record the new, higher pitch level. First, record your prolonged "ah" and then the monotone reading. Listen to the playback. See if you can match (imitate) your own recorded models.

2. Elevating your pitch a note or two is not difficult. It is more natural to raise your speaking pitch a bit more than it is to lower it because you have many more notes available above your habitual pitch than below it.

3. Practice saying these sentences, raising your pitch at the end of the question:

HOW ARE YOU TODAY?

HOW LONG IS THE STORY?

DID YOU POINT YOUR FINGER?

WHERE ARE YOU GOING TO GO NOW?

WHEN WILL THE CONGRESS EVER BE HAPPY?

Practice using the higher pitch by reading aloud in a monotone for a few minutes, several times a day. Practice using the higher pitch in conversation with someone you know well. With some practice, the higher pitch can be part of your new natural voice.

Practice in Varying Your Pitch

Pitch inflection is part of the melody of a language, and makes most languages distinct from one another. Chinese, for example, is a tonal language, with great sweeps in pitch. Some of those pitch changes add different meanings for the same word root. Although some Spanish, Portuguese, and French words look alike when written, it is not just pronunciation that makes them sound different but varying pitch inflections, too. The importance of inflection is even clearer in dialects of the same language. Southerners in the United States, for example, not only pronounce words differently than people in New England do, but the way they stress words of the language is markedly different.

The melody of inflection in the speech of individuals is also part of their distinctive signature when they speak. In English, certain pitch inflections have come to signal certain character traits. For instance, as we point out in later chapters on men's and women's voices, pitch that drops at the end of phrases and sentences (characteristic of men) connotes authority and sureness, while pitch that rises (characteristic of some women) may connote unsureness and shyness.

When we had university students write down words they thought best described the meaning of pitch inflections spoken by past well-known people, the low-pitch inflections of William Buckley were seen as "authoritative, aggressive, in command, decisive, controlling." The rising inflections of Truman Capote were viewed as "effeminate, ambivalent, indecisive, questioning, unsure." In the case of Lyndon Johnson, who lacked good pitch variability, the students wrote, "loss of affect, boredom, no emotionality, fatigued."

Overall, inflections are what give distinctive personality and liveliness to our speech. There is nothing more boring, and eventually irritating, than listening to someone who speaks in a monotone. The normal voice should go up and down around one's natural pitch.

Because lack of pitch inflection, or misplaced speech inflections, can send negative signals about us, most of us can benefit from becoming more critically aware of our habitual pattern of speech inflection. The best way to do this is to listen carefully to our own voices and the voices of those around us.

Record your own voice and the voices of some of the people you hear on television or radio. When you play them back, write down, as our university students did, your impressions of what the voice inflections conveyed to you. Voice changes can be triggered by various emotions (fear, anger, annoyance, etc.). Compare your inflection patterns with those of others you have recorded. If, overall, you rate the others higher or lower than yourself, can you tell what differences in inflection patterns were crucial in making your judgments? What are they doing with their inflections that you don't want to do, or would like to do?

We will show you now some exercises for gaining control over your voice inflections so that you can achieve the pattern you want.

Practice in Rising and Falling Inflections

1. Using the words *well?*, *yes?*, and *no?*, practice rising inflections as shown below.

2. Using the words *go*, *why*, and *no*, practice falling inflections as shown below.

3. Using the words, *no*, *when*, and *yes*, practice double inflections, a rising pitch that falls off to a falling pitch. This kind of pitch bending in a single syllable word seems, as you will hear, to convey sarcasm, uncertainty, or double meaning.

4. You now should have heard how changing the inflection of a word can give that word a special meaning. (This can also be done to some extent by changing your loudness.) Actors and actresses, of course, have refined their talent for using changes in inflection to convey inner feelings. But all of us

do this, consciously or unconsciously, in our daily lives. To gain control over this process, practice the following exercises. Using the word *now*, try to use the word so that it conveys each of the feelings listed.

anger	sad	hopeful	sickly
sarcastic	sexy	scared	happy
defeated	shy	thrilled	disgusted

After you have practiced this for awhile, record your efforts and ask another person to listen to the recording and write down what emotion he or she hears in your voice. Practice this until the word the other person writes down is the word for that emotion you wanted to convey.

5. Finally, you need some exercise in changing pitch inflections not just in single words but in the course of an entire sentence. Read aloud the sentences below, making the pitch changes that are indicated. The words without any marking above or below should be spoken at your natural pitch level. Markings above the word require an upward pitch inflection and the lower markings indicate a lower pitch inflection.

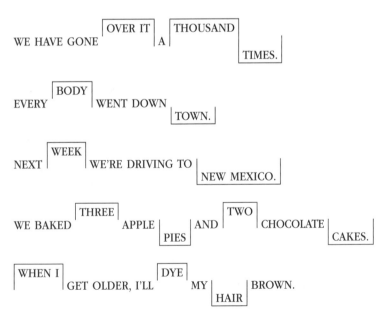

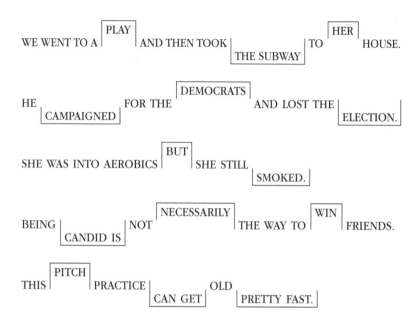

6. After you can read those sentences comfortably, without hesitating, record your reading. What kinds of meaning and emotion do you hear? Now try making different inflections on different words, and write down the different meanings and emotions you hear. You can also try this exercise with sentences of your own or sentences from magazines that you have marked for inflections. In a short time, you will begin to hear that the meaning of a word or a sentence can be dramatically changed with slight changes in inflections.

Pitch is like a facial expression conveyed purely by sound. Imagine saying any of the sentences you have been practicing accompanied by a smile, a frown, a sneer, or a twinkle in your eye. Try this in front of a mirror and you will see that you have profoundly changed the meaning of what you are saying by your accompanying expression.

Pitch changes have the same effect on your speech. A high-pitched voice, a low-pitched one, and a distinctive pattern of inflections all contribute, almost as much as the dictionary definition of the words you are saying, to the meaning and emotional content of your speech.

Changing your pitch level, if it needs to be changed, and gaining control over your pitch inflections, can greatly improve the way you sound and prevent serious misunderstandings. With proper use of pitch, you can say what you mean, and be perceived as always meaning what you say.

CHAPTER 8

Is Your Voice in Focus?

"What you want to avoid is a voice that
sounds as if it's stuck in your throat."

Vocal coaches say that to produce good voice the vocal tract needs to be in focus, just as you need good camera focus for a clear photograph. Of all the voice characteristics that we talk about in this book, focus is the most difficult to describe. It is easy to understand what we mean when we say someone speaks without enough breath, or too high or low in pitch, or too loudly. But what do we mean by good voice focus? With good focus, we mean a voice that sounds as if it is coming from the middle of the mouth, just above the surface of the tongue. The drawing, Figure 8–1, will help you visualize this, a voice focused at the X where lines A and B, the horizontal and vertical planes of the vocal tract, intersect one another.

Another way to make the concept of focus clearer is by describing what bad or poor focus is. Look at the Figure 8–1 illustration. If your voice is produced from a point too high or too low on the vertical line, B, it will have poor vertical focus. Similarly, if your voice is produced too far forward or too far back on the horizontal line, A, it will have poor horizontal focus. The concept of focus will be clearer to you if we "listen" to a couple of cases where focus was poorly used.

Twenty-seven-year-old Rick and his partner Robbie started a wine shop in a fashionable shopping center of a large city. Robbie mostly took care of the back-room chores, the ordering of inventory and keeping the books. Rick was the front man who both partners thought had a gift for dealing with customers.

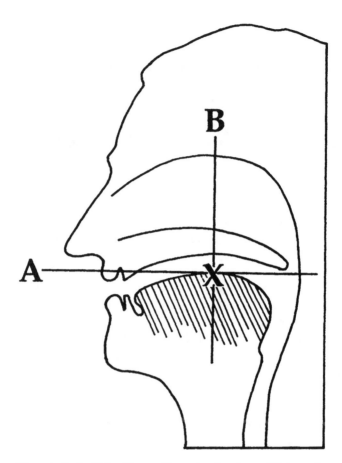

Figure 8–1. Voice Focus. Normal voice focus (X) is at the intersection of line A (horizontal focus) and line B (vertical focus).

The two men had been friends for so long, they took a lot about one another for granted—including the way they spoke. Neither reflected on the fact that, whereas Rick had an engaging personality, he had a high-pitched voice, with a thin front focus, and even a slight frontal lisp, producing a voice that resonated near the tip of his tongue.

They realized they had a problem, however, when it became obvious that when Rick was out front customers didn't linger and didn't buy. But when Robbie filled in at the counter, they made sales. As both partners had staked their life savings on the venture, they took the problem seriously. Rick came to us for voice therapy.

Our goal was to develop exercises that encouraged Rick to use a more posterior carriage of the tongue. We'll show you those exercises later on in this chapter. The horizontal focus exercises worked for Rick. As his tongue came back to a more neutral position, the high, thin voice began to disappear, and so did the severity of his lisp. With this improved horizontal focus, and much practice, Rick developed a nice-sounding baritone voice and the store a steady clientele.

An example of someone with a problem of low vertical focus was Carl, a successful manufacturer's representative in his early 40s. His voice resonated from deep in his throat. He, also, always tried to speak at the very bottom of his pitch range, which compounded the problem. As with so many types of voice misuse, his hoarseness was the symptom that finally got Carl's attention. His hoarseness was so bad that sometimes he hardly had a voice at the end of the day.

When he came to us, our voice evaluation found him to have a normal larynx, throat, and mouth. What he needed was to get his voice out of his throat and into his mouth, so that he might develop a better vertical focus. He was able to do this in his first therapy session. He was a little more resistant to using a higher pitch. Like many men, Carl thought the lower his voice, the more macho he sounded. But when he listened to recorded playbacks, he realized how much better and how clear he sounded with the combination of higher focus and higher pitch. After six weeks of therapy and much self-practice, his hoarseness was totally gone, and whenever Carl needed voice, which was often in his line of work, he had a good one.

Finding the Focus and Balance of the Natural Voice

Let us now look more closely at how one produces both horizontal and vertical focus. Your voice originates in your larynx. As outgoing air from your lungs passes between your two vocal folds, it sets them in vibration. This vibratory sound, you will recall from Chapter 2, is called phonation or voice.

The vibrations set up sound waves that then travel from the larynx into these resonating cavities, your throat, mouth, and nose. The particular shapes and the changing openings of these resonating cavities are what help to give you your distinctive voice. Our unique, basic sound depends to a great extent on how wide open our mouth is, the relative openness of our throat and nose, and the position of our tongue.

Where the tongue is in the mouth contributes to what we call horizontal focus, and strongly affects the sound of our voice. A normal voice has a balanced horizontal focus; the tongue is neither too far forward nor too far back in the mouth. When the tongue is excessively forward, as shown in Figure 8–2, we produce the kind of voice that was such a problem for Rick in

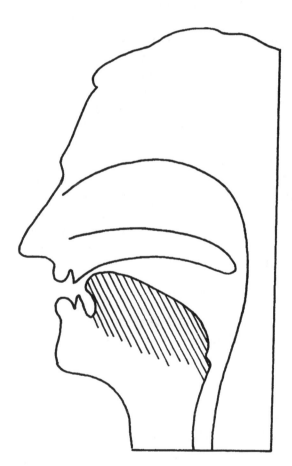

Figure 8–2. Front voice focus.

our first example: voice quality was weak, thin, and in his case contributing to a frontal lisp.

A posterior carriage of the tongue, as seen in Figure 8–3, creates the opposite problem of back oral focus. In extreme cases, for those of you with good memories, the voice may sound like Edgar Bergen's Mortimor Snerd or television's Alf. In both cases, their voice resonance had a back focus. The best horizontal focus resulting in the best voice comes with a tongue carried in the neutral setting in the middle of the mouth.

Vertical focus, on the other hand, doesn't involve tongue placement, but where the voice is produced in relation to the

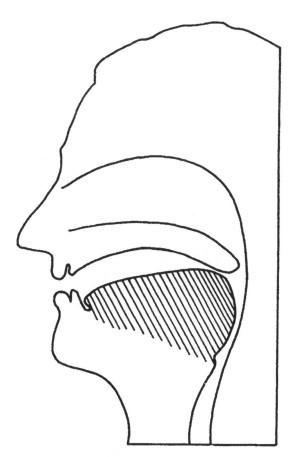

Figure 8–3. Back voice focus.

tongue. Some voices sound locked low in the throat, as was the case with Carl. Other voices sound focused above the tongue, high in the nose. In fact, there are so many people with nasal voices that we will devote a separate chapter, the following one, to the nasality problem. Normal, good voice focus sounds as if the voice bounces off the surface of the tongue in the middle of the mouth, as shown in Figure 8–4.

Your mental image of "placing your voice" in this position is as important to keeping a good vertical focus as the position of your tongue is for horizontal focus.

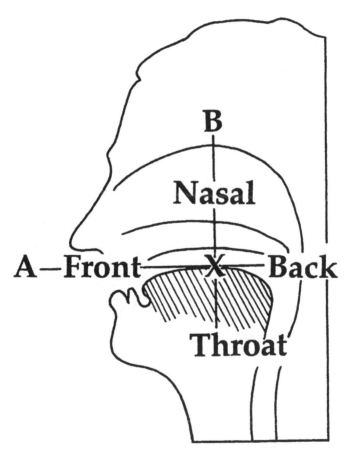

Figure 8–4. Voice focus sites. X = normal.

Test for Voice Focus

Most people have no voice focus problem. If, however, you find that you have a focus problem (front-back-low [throat]-high [nasal]) after taking this brief test, the exercises and suggestions that follow the test can help you develop a more normal sounding voice focus. You will need your recorder. You will also need the list of 100 voice descriptors that you studied in Chapter 1. The list has been reproduced here as Table 8–1 for your use on the Test for Voice Focus. Although you can complete the test wholly on your own, it might be helpful to have a friend help you make some judgments about how your voice sounds.

1. Make a recording reading aloud this passage:

   TO SUCCEED IN LIFE ONE HAS TO BELIEVE IN ONE'S SELF. IT IS VERY EASY TO LET OBSTACLES IN LIFE BECOME ACHIEVEMENT BARRIERS. THIS CAN MAKE US END UP FOCUSING ON WHAT WE CANNOT DO. IT WOULD BE FAR BETTER TO FOCUS ON WHAT WE CAN DO, OR AS STEVE JOBS MIGHT HAVE SAID, "THERE IS NO GREATER TONIC FOR BELIEVING IN ONESELF THAN HAVING SUCCESS."

2. Now ask a friend to help you judge your voice focus. Show him or her the list of 100 word-descriptors for voice. Once you have reviewed the list together, ask your friend to listen to your recording of the paragraph, and then select the ten words from the list that best describe your voice. You, also, should now select ten descriptive words that might describe your voice from the list at the same time.
3. Now compare your list of ten words with your friend's list. If you have normal focus, there is usually less agreement on word choice between you and someone else. If you have a focus problem, you will usually have three or more words that you and another person have agreed on.
4. Using the words that you both agree on, see if you find each word listed in Table 8–2. We have listed the words that typically describe a focus problem under the four out-of-focus headings.

Table 8–1. 100 Word-Descriptors for Voice

___ 1. Abrasive	___ 35. Golden	___ 68. Powerful
___ 2. Affected	___ 36. Good	___ 69. Quiet
___ 3. Aged	___ 37. Gravelly	___ 70. Quivering
___ 4. Angry	___ 38. Happy	___ 71. Relaxed
___ 5. Baby	___ 39. Harmonious	___ 72. Resigned
___ 6. Bad	___ 40. Harsh	___ 73. Resonant
___ 7. Beautiful	___ 41. Heavy	___ 74. Rich
___ 8. Breathy	___ 42. High	___ 75. Ringing
___ 9. Bright	___ 43. Hoarse	___ 76. Rough
___ 10. Brilliant	___ 44. Hollow	___ 77. Sad
___ 11. Bubbly	___ 45. Husky	___ 78. Scratchy
___ 12. Cello-like	___ 46. Immature	___ 79. Sexy
___ 13. Chesty	___ 47. Insecure	___ 80. Shallow
___ 14. Clangy	___ 48. Intimidating	___ 81. Sharp
___ 15. Clear	___ 49. Joyful	___ 82. Silken
___ 16. Coarse	___ 50. Light	___ 83. Smooth
___ 17. Confident	___ 51. Lovely	___ 84. Sophisticated
___ 18. Constricted	___ 52. Low	___ 85. Stentorian
___ 19. Cool	___ 53. Macho	___ 86. Strident
___ 20. Covered	___ 54. Masculine	___ 87. Sultry
___ 21. Cutting	___ 55. Mature	___ 88. Thin
___ 22. Dark	___ 56. Mellow	___ 89. Throaty
___ 23. Decisive	___ 57. Melodious	___ 90. Tight
___ 24. Deep	___ 58. Metallic	___ 91. Timid
___ 25. Dry	___ 59. Monotone	___ 92. Tired
___ 26. Dull	___ 60. Nasal	___ 93. Ugly
___ 27. Effeminate	___ 61. Nervous	___ 94. Unsure
___ 28. Edgy	___ 62. Normal	___ 95. Velvety
___ 29. Fearful	___ 63. Old	___ 96. Warm
___ 30. Flat	___ 64. Open	___ 97. Wavering
___ 31. Feminine	___ 65. Pinched	___ 98. Wet
___ 32. Fluttering	___ 66. Pleasing	___ 99. Whining
___ 33. Forced	___ 67. Poor	___ 100. Whiskey
___ 34. Friendly		

Table 8–2. Words That Typically Describe a Focus Problem

Front	Back	Throat	Nasal
abrasive	cello-like	angry	clangy
baby	covered	chesty	cutting
brilliant	dark	decisive	harsh
constricted	flat	deep	high
effeminate	friendly	forced	metallic
fearful	hollow	gravelly	nasal
feminine	open	heavy	pinched
immature	resonant	hoarse	ringing
joyful	sad	husky	sharp
light	silken	low	strident
nervous	stentorian	macho	whining
old	velvety	masculine	
shallow		rough	
thin		sultry	
timid		throaty	
unsure		wet	
		whiskey	

5. If you find three or more of the words that you and your friend agreed on in the same column, you probably have that particular focus problem. If there are only one or two words in one column or most words are scattered across the columns, you probably do not have an obvious focus problem.

If you feel that you have a voice focus problem but were unable to identify it clearly (you did not have three or more words in the same column), you may wish to consult a speech-language pathologist (see Chapter 16). If you found that your voice may have a front or back or low or high focus, practicing the appropriate exercises that follow may help you.

Exercises for Changing Your Voice Focus

Correcting Front (Anterior) Focus

Excessive front focus comes from carrying the tongue too far forward. Front-of-the-mouth focus can, however, be corrected with some back-focus practice on the following exercises.

1. Practice making the isolated *k* and *g* sounds. Using these back sounds can often correct a front voice focus:

   KUH   KUH   KAH   KAH
   GUH   GUH   GAH   GAH

   The consonants *k* and *g* are made with the tip of the tongue down and the back of the tongue arched up against the roof of the mouth or posterior palate. They are back-in-the-mouth sounds. Just saying them in a slightly exaggerated manner will often eliminate the front-of-the-mouth sound of your voice.

2. Practice prolonging the vowels in each of these *k* and *g* sounding words. You should begin to feel the back focus of the voice as you say them:

   KEEP   KEY   KOOK   COKE   COOK   COD
   COMB   CORN   CAR   CULT   COME   GO
   GOAT   GOD   GUARD   GUILT   GULCH   GOT GUM

3. Now practice reading aloud the *k* and *g* sentences below, keeping the voice back. This time record your reading so you may listen to the playback when you finish:

   CANDY CANES CRUMBLED AT CHRISTMAS.

   THE CONSERVATION WAS GOOD AND CANDID.

   CAROLE HAD A CALORIE COUNTER ON THE CANNISTER.

   COUNTRY COUSINS CAME TO THE CORN SHOW.

   CARL FOUND A CARBON COPY OF THE CABIN CRUISER.

   GREAT GRANDMOTHER GROUND THE COFFEE BEANS.

   FROM THE BIG LEAGUES GROVER WENT INTO BIG GOVERNMENT.

HE GRABBED UP THE GREEN GRAPES FROM THE GRAPE COUNTER

THE ALLIGATOR FEARED THE BEAGLE GUIDE DOG COULD GRAB HIM.

THE GOOD GOVERNOR'S SHAG RUG IS NO LONGER GOLD AND GRAY.

4. Listen to the playback. By now your voice should have less anterior focus. If you can, read a few of the sentences in your old voice, then say a few in your middle-of-the-mouth voice.
5. Can you feel the difference? Can you hear the difference?

If the above steps have not helped you enough to develop a voice with less front focus, repeat all the steps, and drop your pitch one note as you do the exercises. Lowering the voice one note may contribute to reducing front voice focus.

Correcting Back (Posterior) Focus

Because the tongue is so far back in the mouth, speakers with a back focus often lack clarity of speech articulation. The exercises to develop more front focus are the opposite of those for developing back focus, and are designed to bring the tongue farther forward. Try the following:

1. Say each of the words below in an abrupt whisper (do not use voice).

PEEP PIPE PEACH PEAS PEAT PIE PATCH

The *p* sound is made by pursing the lips, filling the cheeks with air, and suddenly releasing it.

THIS THAT THIN THINK THICK THIGH THATCH

The *th* sound is made by sticking the tongue out between the upper and lower front teeth as you make the sound.

SEE SAT SIN SINK SICK SIGH SEAT

The *s* sound is made by placing the tip of the tongue on the gum ridge behind the upper front teeth as you make the sound.

2. Now say each of the previous words, first in a whisper and then quickly with voice. Your voice should feel and sound more forward than back.

3. Elevate your voice pitch by one note and try reading the sentences below in the higher pitch. Record your reading.

   TEACHERS EAT RIPE PEACHES AT THE BEACH.

   PETE BOUGHT AN APPLE PIE AT THE BABY BAKERY.

   THE THISTLES SPRANG UP BY THE PINE TREE FOREST.

   THEY ATE PEACH AND RASPBERRY TARTS AT THE TABLE.

   PEOPLE THAT BUY BIG SUVS PAY MORE AT THE PUMP.

   THERE MUST BE FIVE OR SIX PEACH TREE STREETS.

   THE BIG ELECTRIC TYPEWRITER WAS REPLACED BY A WORD PROCESSOR.

   THEY BOUGHT A WREATH OF PINK ROSES FOR THE PROFESSOR.

   STOCK PRICES WENT UP BEFORE WE SOLD OUR PIPE STOCKS.

   THE PEOPLE WANT TO PAY FOR BIGGER SPACE EXPLORATION.

4. Listen to your recording of the sentences. When you recorded them you should have felt the words spoken in the front of the mouth. By now your voice should sound focused more in the mouth than in the back of your throat.

5. Select a paragraph or two from a book or magazine. Read it aloud in what you think is your new voice, with more front focus. Then, if you can, read it in your old way with back-in-the-throat focus. Can you feel the difference? Now read the material again, recording it, but this time read it once with what you think is front focus and then with what you think is back focus. You should be able to hear the difference on playback.

Correcting Throat Focus

The person with poor vertical focus, who appears to "speak in the throat," places unnecessary strain on the larynx. Correcting the problem requires a good mental image of where the voice is coming from, and using focusing exercises to help place it up where you want it to be:

1. Try saying "EAT A BITE OF PIE," back in your mouth, then deep in your throat, and then high in your nose. If you can make those focus changes with relative ease, you should be able to "lift" your voice to where it should be, toward the surface of the middle of your tongue.
2. Record your attempts to move your focus around like this, every now and then using your old, low-throat voice. You should hear a marked contrast between the balanced voice coming from the middle of the mouth and the low-throat voice. Practice using the balanced voice until it becomes habitual. If you cannot do this with relative ease, try the following steps.
3. Make a very nasal voice, placing your voice high up in your nasal cavities. This is only a temporary step to get your voice out of your throat. Now, in an exaggerated nasal voice, say:

MANY-MANY-MANY

MAN-OH-MAN-OH-MAN

MONEY-MONEY-MONEY

RINGING-RINGING-RINGING

As you say these words nasally, place your fingers on the bridge of your nose. You should be able to feel the vibrations of the nasal cartilages as you speak. To further experience this high nasal focus, say the following phrases aloud:

MAN IN THE MOON

MANY MEN WANT MORE MONEY

NEVER WANT ONE TIME ONLY

MORNING SUN MAKES THE MORNING

4. What you have been producing is a high nasal, vertical focus higher than you want. But it brought your voice out of your throat. What you need to do now is to bring your voice to the target focus area that was shown you in Figure 8–4. Think of the X area in that drawing as in your own mouth. Try to say

the following words with your voice focused in your mind to be at that X:

RASPBERRY PATCH

PEACH TREE PLAZA

EAT A BITE OF PIE

PETE'S BABY BAKERY

5. Record your reading of the exercises in steps 3 and 4 and listen to the playback. You should hear a sharp contrast between the two focus points, nasal and middle of the mouth. If you cannot hear the difference at first, repeat steps 3 and 4. Once you have heard the difference, try reading and recording the following passage with your voice placed at the X-focus site:

THERE ARE MANY SATELLITES CIRCLING THE EARTH. SOME HAVE BEEN PLACED IN ORBIT BY THE SPACE SHUTTLE, WHILE OTHERS HAVE BEEN BLASTED INTO ORBIT BY LAUNCHED ROCKETS. EVENTUALLY, THE SATELLITES WILL BE SERVICED AT SPACE STATIONS WHICH WILL ALSO BE CIRCLING THE EARTH AT VARIOUS ORBITAL ALTITUDES.

Listen to the playback. Is your focus where it should be? If it is, you are well on your way to being able consistently to get your voice out of your throat.

6. Remember that a major part of good vertical focus depends on imagery. We cannot physically place the voice anywhere. But by focusing on a mental image on a physical site in the vocal tract, we can produce a marked difference in the sound of our voice. Keep that picture of the X-focus site in Figure 8–4 in your mind. Summon its imagery up before you speak. If you do this, speaking in the middle of your mouth on the surface of your tongue may well become second nature to you.

7. Good vertical focus requires a good ear as well as good imagery. Most of you probably have found that you used the imagery well and have brought your voice out of your throat. You can hear the results on the playbacks of your

recordings. But if, after going through these steps a second time, you still have a throat focus, you might want to contact a speech-language pathologist (see Chapter 16).

Correcting Nasal Focus

Good imagery is important to your being able to locate and sustain good voice focus. And good voice focus is equally important to the vocal image of yourself that you project to others. With the concept of focus now in mind, think back to the voices of the famous people we talked about in Chapter 1. The best of the voices, in addition to other positive qualities, have excellent focus. Focus is a major part of what gives their voices clarity and assurance, and what enables them to project their voices with no audible sign of effort. Despite the improvements you have made so far in your breathing, loudness control, and pitch, you still require good focus to project your voice both naturally and attractively.

If you found in your search for voice focus that there appeared to be a nasal focus to your voice, the next chapter, Talking Through Your Nose, should be of some help.

CHAPTER 9

Talking Through Your Nose

"Her irritating nasal voice went away after she worked on it."

Although a mildly nasal voice can be tolerated fairly well by most people who have to listen to it, excessive nasality often costs a speaker a lot in both business and social situations. A nasal voice is unattractive to many listeners and can become irritating if we have to listen to it for too long.

Like many voice problems, nasality is something the speaker may be aware that he or she has to some extent, but may be unaware of just how bad it really sounds and, worst of all, may assume that nothing can be done about it.

That was the case with Maggie, who at 35 was a sales representative for a paper goods manufacturer in a major sales market. Maggie had always been in sales. She attributed the fact that she had changed jobs and product lines often, consistent with the nomadic habits of many sales people. But there was another pattern to Maggie's job switching. She began each position with fair success, but then experienced a slow, steady loss of customers. She began to have trouble scheduling appointments; more of her phone calls found her clients "busy," and they returned her calls less and less.

"Why doesn't anyone want to talk to me anymore?" she complained to her sales manager. In response, she got the best critique of her career. "Maybe the problem is that they don't want to listen to you," he said.

That was what brought Maggie to us. We heard her consistent nasality at once and suspected it was the source of her problem. Testing showed that the cause of her nasality was not physical. Her mouth, throat, and soft palate were normal. The movements of her soft palate were normal, allowing her to close off her nose from her mouth when she wanted to do so. We were quickly able to demonstrate that she had the physical capability to have normal voice resonance.

We then gave her some voice models, free of nasality, to imitate which she was able to do. We recorded the results, and compared them to an old voice recording that she had first brought to our office. Maggie was amazed. She knew that she spoke nasally, but she had never known how bad it sounded. In fact, she told us, like a great many people, even in this high-tech age, that she had never heard a recording of her own voice.

A voice therapy program was started that enabled her to make good oral resonance as a normal, natural part of her speaking. In three months her voice was free of excessive nasality. It turned out that Maggie had a very attractive natural voice to go with her outgoing personality. And her customers were happy both to talk to her and to listen to her.

Before we continue, we need to point out that Maggie's problem was one of two kinds of problems that people have with nasality. Her case was one of *hypernasality,* the familiar whining or twanging voice that seems to come out of the nose. Some people, although far fewer, have the opposite problem, *denasality,* where there is insufficient nasal resonance.

The causes and treatment of each type of nasal problem are very different, and we will examine them in more detail in a moment. But let's look at the problem of denasality.

Howard, 36, was a first officer flying "right chair" for a major airline. Among flight crews, Howard was continually kidded about sounding most of the time as if he had a severe head cold. He spoke in a muffled voice that was hard to understand, lacking nasal resonance for the three nasal sounds in English that need it, the *m, n,* and *ng.*

Comments on his voice from air controllers and passengers, however, were not kidding. For the former, not being able to understand Howard was serious. In the case of the passengers, it was frustrating, irritating, and, in the case of nervous passengers, probably alarming.

More often than with cases of hypernasality, denasality can come from physical causes, such as large adenoids high in the throat that block the free passage of air and sound waves flowing through the nose. People who have trouble breathing through their noses often turn out to have such a physical problem.

We found, however, that Howard's problem was functional, not physical. For whatever reasons, he carried his tongue so far back in his mouth that he shut off the air passages to his nose. His voice resonated more in his throat than in either his nose or mouth. Most of the time, he also seemed to speak at the very bottom of his pitch range.

All of the things he had been doing to produce his back voice were corrected by voice therapy. He used the exercises presented in Chapter 8 for developing better oral focus. The pitch raising exercises shown in Chapter 7 helped him raise his speaking pitch a couple of notes. His denasality was helped by following the exercises at the end of this chapter for reducing denasality. Howard's voice greatly improved, allowing him to give much clearer cockpit radio responses and clearer instructions to his passengers. He called recently to tell us that both his airline career and private life had improved greatly "since getting my voice out of my throat."

Let us look now at the causes of both hypernasality and denasality. Then we will give you tests for both kinds of problems and show you some exercises to correct them.

Hypernasality

Only the three nasal sounds, *m, n,* and *ng,* receive their primary resonance within the nose and nasal cavities. All the other sounds of English are diverted into the mouth where they receive their primary resonance. The sounds of the usual normal voice coming up from the vibrating vocal folds are diverted by the soft palate into the mouth. In Figure 9–1, we see a line drawing of the palate-throat closing mechanism. In this side view of the

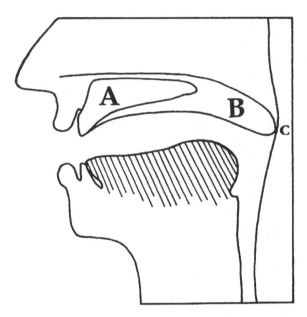

Figure 9–1. The normal closed palate-throat mechanism. Voice comes out the mouth.

mouth, we see the bony hard palate (A) with the soft muscular soft palate (B) touching the back wall of the throat or pharynx (C). The oral cavity is clearly separated from the nasal cavity.

In Figure 9–2, we see the normal open palate. While breathing in and out through the nose, the soft palate (B) is relaxed and hanging down, allowing airflow and sound waves to travel into the nose. When speaking, this down position of the soft palate only occurs for the nasal resonance of *m, n,* and *ng.* During normal speech, the soft palate continually lifts up and touches the throat wall near the point C in the drawing. This elevation of the soft palate shuts off the mouth from the nose, and diverts the sound waves from the vocal folds into the mouth. Thus, voice resonance is in the mouth and throat, below the closure point B–C.

In normal voice, the closure point opens only for the nasal resonance of the sounds *m, n,* and *ng.* In cases of hypernasality, however, it remains open and all voice sounds are given some nasal resonance.

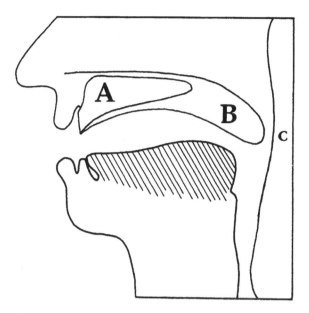

Figure 9–2. The normal open palate-throat mechanism. Voice comes out the nose.

Hypernasality can have physical causes, among them a physically short palate, a cleft palate, or weakened palatal muscles. If you think your hypernasality has a physical cause, you should find sources for help among the specialists listed in Chapter 16.

In this book, we are concerned with those of you whose hypernasality has a functional cause, as was the case with Maggie. The upcoming Tests for Nasality will help you determine if you have hypernasality, and if the problem can be eliminated with exercises, or perhaps requiring specialized professional treatment.

Denasality

In denasality the sound waves of the voice cannot get into nasal cavities to resonate for those *m, n,* and *ng* sounds; in addition, some of the vowel sounds and even the oral consonants may be slightly denasalized. The resulting voice sounds like someone speaking with a head cold, and as was the case with Howard, other people often have difficulty understanding what is said.

More often than not, denasality has a physical cause. In Figure 9–3, we show such a blockage. In this side view, we see excessive tissue (like adenoids and tonsils) in the area of the pharyngeal wall (C). Even though the soft palate (B) may be dropped and open, there is so much tissue between B and C that sound waves cannot get into the nasal cavities.

Some problems of denasality, however, do not have such a physical cause and can be helped with speech-voice exercises. Our Tests for Nasality will tell you if your resonance problem is denasality. If it is, you might first want to try some of the suggestions that follow for reducing the problem. If the problem persists, regardless of what you try to do, you might want to consult one of the ear-nose-throat specialists listed in Chapter 16.

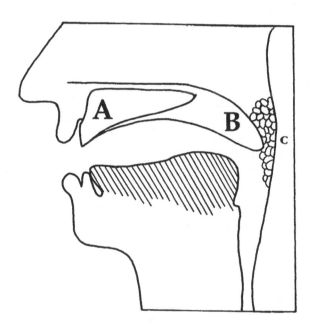

Figure 9–3. Tissue, like large adenoids, prevents closure of the soft palate (B) against the pharyngeal wall (C), causing denasality.

Tests for Nasality

There are two tests here, the first to determine if you have a problem of hypernasality and the second to find if you have a problem of denasality. If you are uncertain as to which problem you have, take both tests. Neither will take long. The only equipment you need for each test is a recorder, such as a smartphone, that can provide audio playback.

Test for Hypernasality

Read aloud and record the two passages below. Each passage has no nasal consonants.

> EACH YEAR, EARTH SATELLITES BLAST AWAY TOWARD OUTER SPACE. THEY FLY TOWARD THE BLACK HOLE OF SPACE TO JUPITER WITH ITS CLOUDS OF ICE CRYSTALS.

> BETTY WAS BOB'S BIG SISTER. SHE TOOK BOB TO THE ICE SHOW EVERY SATURDAY BY BUS. IT TOOK OVER TWO HOURS BY BUS TO REACH THE BIG CITY.

Still recording, read the passages again. But this time squeeze your nostrils closed as you begin the second sentence and continue to read aloud.

Assessing the Test Results

1. There are no nasal consonants in either of these reading passages. Consequently, on playback you should hear no nasality in your reading. If after you squeezed your nostrils closed there was no change in your voice resonance, you do not have hypernasality. Listen carefully to your recording again. If there was no change in the sound of your voice whether your nostrils were open or closed, you do not have hypernasality.
2. If after squeezing your nostrils closed there was a noticeable change in your resonance, or occasionally all voicing

stopped, you have hypernasality. The exercises presented later in this chapter may be able to help you develop normal resonance.

Test for Denasality

Read aloud and record the two passages below. The passages are loaded with nasal consonants.

MAN IS FINDING MANY MOONS AROUND DISTANT PLANETS. IN MANY PLANETARY SYSTEMS, MANY MOONS ARE FOUND AROUND THE NUMEROUS PLANETS.

DAN AND TOM WENT TO TOM'S GRANDMOTHER'S FARM. ON MANY NIGHTS ON THE FARM, THE MAN IN THE MOON SEEMED TO SHINE DOWN ON THEM.

Still recording, read the same passage again. But this time squeeze your nostrils closed as you begin the second sentence and continue reading aloud.

Assessing the Test Results

1. Both passages contain an unusual number of nasal consonants. Therefore, on the first playback, when you did not squeeze off your nostrils, the normal voice should sound quite nasal. When you squeeze off your nostrils, the normal voice will either stop completely or there will be a marked change in your nasal resonance. This would be the normal response for a voice free of denasality.
2. If you have denasality, the two recordings will sound similar. Because in denasality there is little normal nasal resonance in your voice, very little air or sound is passing through your nose when you produce *m*, *n*, and *ng*. Consequently, when you squeeze off your nose, if you are denasal, it will make very little difference in the way that you sound. Little or no change in voice resonance on both readings (with and without nasal pinching) shows that you are denasal, and that you might profit from the exercises for denasality presented later in this chapter.

Exercises for Developing a Proper Balance of Oral and Nasal Resonance

You now have discovered whether you have a problem of hypernasality or denasality (or no problem with nasality at all, in which case you can go on to the next chapter). The person with hypernasality will have too much nasal resonance and not enough oral resonance. The person with denasality will not resonate the nasal *m, n,* and *ng* sounds, which may influence some adjacent oral sounds as well.

The exercises that follow are designed to help you develop the right balance of oral and nasal resonance in your natural voice. They may even be useful to those of you whose problems with nasality are slight. In contrast to the examples we have used for purposes of illustration, many people are only slightly nasal or slightly denasal, and they could improve the sound of their natural voices with just a little effort.

Practice Exercises for Hypernasality

1. Lower your voice pitch a note. If you have been speaking at too high a pitch, lowering your voice to a more natural level often permits your whole vocal tract to function more efficiently. To do this, use the exercises for lowering pitch that were given in Chapter 7.
2. Reduce the loudness of your voice. A softer voice will often sound less nasal. Also, at a softer loudness level a nasal voice is less irritating to listeners. To reduce your loudness, try the exercises given in Chapter 6.
3. There should be no in nasal resonance when you say words that have no nasal consonants with your nostrils open or squeezed closed. Words with all oral consonants have no nasal resonance. Practice good oral resonance by saying the words slightly louder that are listed below:

BEACH   PIG   BAKE   PORCH

PEAT   BACK   TAKE   BOOK

BITCH   PATCH   BARK   PUSH

- Read aloud each of the above words, one at a time, prolonging the vowel sound so the word is prolonged as you say it.
- Now record a second reading of the words. As you do, pinch off your nostrils now and then. If you do have hypernasality when your nose is pinched off you will hear a marked difference in the sound of your voice.
- If you can hear no change in your voice when you close off your nostrils, you are saying the words free of nasality. This is good. Keep up this kind of practice.
- If you hear any change in your voice when your nostrils are pinched closed, or if your voice is stopped, you still have too much nasal resonance and should go on to the next step.

4. Become aware of the movement of your soft palate.

- In front of a mirror or video, yawn with a wide-open mouth, breathing through your nose. Look inside your open mouth. Note the dangling uvula hanging from your soft palate at the back of your mouth.
- Say "AAAAAAAH" prolonging the sound. As you do, notice how your soft palate and uvula rise. At the end of the word, you will see that the soft palate drops down to the open position, lowering the uvula.
- Now say "AAAAAAANG" (rhymes with sang), prolonging the sound. Notice that the soft palate and the uvula stay down. This allows the sound waves to resonate in your nose.
- Now say five "ah" words with your mouth wide open. Pause a second or two between each word. In the mirror or on video playback, you will see that the soft palate and uvula go up for each word, and drop down during the pause.

This exercise has shown you how to produce normal oral resonance. The soft palate goes up to shut off the nose from the oral cavity. When we make nasal sounds the palate drops down so that the voice can be resonated above in the nasal cavities.

5. Let us take another look at the function of the soft palate, this time using a hand mirror.

   • Place the mirror directly under your nostrils. Say a prolonged "AAAAAAAH." If the sound has normal oral resonance, the mirror will not cloud as there is no outflowing air coming from your nose.

   • Keeping the mirror in place, say a prolonged "MAAAAAAAN." As you do, you should notice the mirror cloud over from the warm, moist air flowing out of your nose.

   • Say the following oral words with the mirror in place. If your voice is free of hypenasality, there will be no clouding of the mirror.

   BEACH   TAKE   COURT

   PITCH   DAYS   GOLD

   • Say the following nasal words with the mirror in place. Now you should see clouding of the mirror as you say each word as air passes out of the nose.

   MEAN   NAME   SONG

   MINE   NONE   RING

6. If you said the six oral words with no clouding of the mirror, see if you can make a contrast between an oral word and a nasal word. You no longer need to use the mirror. Record these pairs of words and see if you can hear a difference on playback.

TEA	KNEE	BOAT	NOTE
BET	NET	BOOK	NOOK
TAIL	NAIL	TOT	NOT
BILE	MILE	BEAR	MARE
TASK	MASK	TOYS	NOISE

   When you can say these contrasting words and easily hear the difference between oral and nasal resonance on playback, you are ready to do some oral reading practice.

7. Go back to the Tests for Nasality. Record your reading of the all oral passage. On playback, does your resonance sound

normal? If you still hear some hypernasality, repeat the first six steps of these practice materials. If what you hear sounds normal to you, reinforce your progress by reading and recording the sentences below, which have no nasal consonants.

WE WISH TO SEE THE BLACK PIRATE SHIPS BY THE DOCK.

SHE ATE COTTAGE CHEESE WITH BISCUITS FOR BREAKFAST.

I BELIEVE THE CUP OF BLACK COFFEE HIT THE SPOT.

WE DUG A HOLE FOR THE CASH BY THE GRAVE YARD.

HE WROTE THE BAD BOY A CHECK FOR FIFTY DOLLARS.

JACK TOOK JILL UP THE HILL TO LOOK AT THE VIEW, OR SO THEY SAY.

HE TRIED TO HAVE THE RAW COURAGE TO STOP THE BLOOD.

THEY TOOK THE SOLDIERS BACK TO THE SAILOR'S HOSPITAL.

If your oral reading sounds free of nasality, keep practicing with any reading material that you wish. What you need at this point is continuous practice until the proper balance of oral and nasal resonance becomes second nature to you. If none of the preceding steps have helped your voice, you may need to consult some of the specialists listed in Chapter 16.

Practice Exercises for Denasality

If you found that your voice resonance was denasal on the Tests for Nasality, it is important for you to find out whether the condition is caused by physical blockage or is functional (something you are doing). The following screening test will enable you to determine this.

Screening Test for Denasality

Take in a bigger than normal breath through your nose. Close your mouth and let the air slowly out your nose. As the nasal air is flowing, press your left nostril closed by your finger. Does the air then flow through the open right nostril? Release the left nostril and press shut the right nostril. Does the air divert through the left nostril? Do this a few times to be certain of the results.

If there is some kind of blockage, little air will flow through one or both nostrils. This could be caused by enlarged adenoids, swelling from allergies, or a number of other causes that need to be pursued medically (see Chapter 16). If there is some kind of structural blockage, the exercises below will not help. But, if you have found that you have good passage of air in and out of the nostrils, yet still sound denasal, the exercises below may help you develop normal resonance.

1. Speak in a slightly higher pitch. Elevate your pitch one note, as described in Chapter 7. If the higher pitch improves your resonance, practice some oral reading using the higher pitch. Record your readings so that you can listen to your resonance critically.
2. Increase the loudness of your voice. Increasing your loudness requires greater airflow and air pressure, and this alone can help you increase your nasality. Use the exercises described in Chapter 6 for increasing your loudness.
3. Ear training is sometimes helpful for increasing nasality. For someone with a problem of denasality, *m* may sound like *b*, *n* sounds like *d*, and *ng* may sound like *g*. Ask someone with normal resonance to record the following pairs of words that denasal people often have problems with.

MAY	BAY	MAT	BAT
ME	BEE	MILK	BILK
MET	BET	MOAT	BOAT
MEAT	BEET	MORE	BORE
MY	BYE	MUST	BUST
NEED	BEAD	BING	BIG
NIP	DIP	BANG	BAG
NINE	DINE	BRING	BRIG
NO	DOUGH	RANG	RAG
NOR	DOOR	TANG	TAG

This discrimination exercise should let you hear the difference between a nasal word and an oral word when you play back the recording. Can you hear the difference? Ask the person making the recording to say just one of the words from some of the pairs. On playback, can you hear which of the words was said?

Now read and record the word pairs and the single words yourself and listen to yourself in the same critical way.

4. Try this humming exercise. Prolong an "AH" and then close your lips while you say it. The sound should then go through your nose. This is the "emmmmmmm" or humming sound.

- Prolong the humming *m*. Place your fingers on the bridge of your nose as you do. You should feel the nasal vibrations.
- Now prolong an *n* sound so that it comes out as "ennnnnnnn." Open your lips and place your tongue behind your upper teeth as you do. Prolong the sound as long as you can, and check the vibrations in your nose with your fingers. These vibrations represent the nasality you want to add to your voice.
- Now prolong the *ng* sound in the word "rang" and stretching it out as long as you can. Again feel your nose vibrations with your fingers.

With some practice you will soon be able to feel, even without having to check with your fingers, when the sounds you make have nasal vibrations and when they do not. This will make it easier for you to get normal nasal resonance on the words and sounds that require it.

5. If you have been successful thus far in getting some nasal sound, practice reading aloud, while recording, the two passages below that contain many nasal sounds. Make your voice extra nasal as you read, checking the vibrations in your nose with your fingers if you have to.

ON A CLEAR NIGHT, DAN AND TOM COULD SEE THE MAN IN THE MOON. ON TOM'S GRANDMOTHER'S FARM, THERE WERE MANY NIGHTS WHEN THERE WAS NO SMOKE AND SMOG. DAN AND TOM WOULD COME TO THE FARM ON MANY MOONLIT NIGHTS TO SEE THE MOON.

MAN IS FINDING MANY MOONS AROUND NUMEROUS PLANETS. IN SOME SOLAR SYSTEMS, THERE ARE NUMEROUS MOONS CIRCLING MANY OF THE DISTANT PLANETS THAT ARE ORBITING AROUND THEIR OWN SUN.

If you have been able to increase nasality in your voice, you now need to spend time practicing reading and speaking with that increased nasal resonance. Use any newspaper, magazine, or book for practice until you feel that you have the proper nasal resonance whenever you want it. Check your voice from time to time with your recorder.

Again, if your denasality has not improved, it may well be related to some kind of structural blockage; and you should consult an otolaryngologist (ear-nose-throat doctor).

A normal, natural voice has the proper balance between nasal and oral resonance. In the English language we need to be able to make both kinds of sounds. To speak properly, and intelligibly, we need control over these sounds so that they are not confused with one another. Hypernasality is a far more common problem than denasality, but denasality can be just as hard on those who have to listen to it. Fortunately, in most cases, we have found that both conditions can be corrected.

CHAPTER 10

Your Emotions and Your Voice

"I couldn't let my passengers hear any fear in my voice."

Our emotions just happen. They happen spontaneously and can often be heard in our voices and seen on our faces. Our emotions are often reactions to stress that can trigger either positive emotions (such as happy) or negative reactions (such as angry). Because of the spontaneous onset of emotions, they are difficult to study and describe. Some actors can portray different emotions well, but research tells us that portrayals do not produce the same kind of physiologic or internal changes that real or spontaneous emotions produce. Likewise, it is difficult under laboratory conditions required for study to produce stress conditions that will prompt positive or negative emotions.

All of us experience various stresses in our daily lives that are often strong enough to produce emotional reactions. Although there is some medical evidence that expression of our emotions is good for one's overall body function, it ignores the impact that your emotional reactions to stress may cause stressful reactions on someone listening to you.

The term *stress* was popularized a few years ago by Hans Selye in his classic book, *Stress Without Distress* (1974). After years of studying stress and stress reactions in his laboratory in Vienna, Selye concluded that "stress is the nonspecific response of the body to any demand made upon it." More simply, stress produces an overstimulation of the body.

Contrary to the popular view that stress causes only negative experiences, Selye wrote that stress can come from either pleasant or unpleasant experiences. Voice can be altered by either pleasant or negative emotions. Great elation and positive excitement can make noticeable changes in your voice. Similarly, emotional reactions to sad news can be heard in dramatic changes in voice. Stage fright, for example, which we deal with separately in the next chapter, might be described as both a pleasant and unpleasant experience, both exhilarating but anxiety-producing. Both type emotions can have an adverse effect on voice as well as negative effects on the listener. For example, after winning a women's tennis final in a grand slam, the thrilled winner yelled excessively as she skipped around the tennis court. The losing girl later reported that both the loud voice and the celebration skipping had great negative effects on her, requiring several weeks to find her competitive balance again.

People experience stress in unexpected situations. Like the tennis star above, the loser experienced more stress after the match than she probably did during the match. Or one can experience positive stress from unexpected joy that might come from winning a contest or winning an award for some kind of outstanding performance. Receiving exceptional compliments from someone may make it difficult to make some kind of normal spoken response. The pure joy of standing in a wedding reception line can raise such positive emotions that a proud parent cannot find the voice to converse with congratulating family and friends.

Negative stress situations commonly produce emotional voice situations. Emotions prompted by the grief of losing a child in an accident can make it difficult for parents at a funeral service to speak with other mourners. Perhaps the most negative emotion affecting one's voice is anger. The anger response has an immediate lowering of voice pitch in a loud voice. Voicing such anger can have frightening effects on nearby listeners. Negative emotions can also come from such frustrations as being stuck in traffic, or from unwanted listening to someone's loud music in the background where you work.

The title of this book, *Is Your Voice Telling on You?*, asks an important question. Some of the time and in the right situations, letting your emotions show in your voice is probably a healthy thing to do. Sometimes, it might be better to reduce the severity of your vocal reactions to an emotion for two reasons: (1) it reduces the strain on your voice and (2) it is less likely to have negative impact on your listeners. We recently treated a retired airline captain (Captain Eric) for voice therapy, and this is how he recorded our question on voice and emotional control:

> In over thirty years flying both domestic and international, I became aware of the effect of emotions on my voice. The "ups and downs" of short domestic hops was hardest of all. I never talked to passengers until we were well airborne after take-off. Take-off is always a tense time and you could usually hear it in the voices of the cockpit crew. Once you're up there cruising at 30,000 feet on auto-pilot, things are relaxed, and I always had a great voice then for talking to my passengers. Since landing was more of a stress builder, you talked to your passengers only at the very beginning of your descent. I couldn't let my passengers hear any fear in my voice, so I was always quiet on final approach. That's a tense time until your wheels touch and you hit your reverse thrust to slow-down your landing speed. And what a great relaxed voice I had after landing and welcoming the folks to Dallas or some place as we taxied to the gate.

His awareness of how negative emotion could be heard in his voice was in sharp contrast to the absence of such emotions allowing him to use his normal voice. Captain Eric's narrative about voice and emotion illustrates two ways anyone can use to avoid emotional voice situations: (1) if possible, avoid exposure to situations that trigger emotion; and (2) when excessive emotion hits, take the option of being silent. When one wishes to speak again, control of emotions becomes a bit more complicated.

Most of the time, our emotions are suddenly experienced and our verbal emotional responses are expressed almost simultaneously. Interesting research of studies on emotion using MRI at the time of emotion onset and verbal responses show that the words we say seem to be automatically driven by the left hemisphere of the brain. The words we often hear may be severe and profane beyond one's control. Images of the brain using MRI show that the emotional voice that comes with the words appears to have right hemisphere origins. After one's immediate reaction to an emotion, one can often begin to modify his or her response. The point is this, the immediate emotional response to an unexpected emotion cannot be easily modified; however, in the following pages, as the intensity of the emotion "calms down," we will show you some things you can do to change the sound of your emotional voice. Also, these voice tips can help most of us use a more natural voice in stressful situations. Listed here alphabetically are some voice difficulties that can be reduced by using a few voice therapy methods:

- dry mouth and throat
- harshness
- high pitch
- hoarseness (dysphonia)
- low pitch
- monotone
- no voice (aphonia)
- pitch breaks
- shortness of breath
- strained voice
- voice breaks
- weak voice

Methods for Keeping Your Natural Voice Under Stress

Dry Throat and Mouth

A typical reaction to excessive negative stress is a dry mouth and throat. If humidity levels in a room or office can be increased, this can help. A good humidity level for a normal voice is 30% to 40%. Situational dryness of the mouth and throat, often related to anxiety, can be minimized by the following strategies:

1. Moving your tongue across your teeth and biting down gently on your tongue as it moves around the mouth. This increases salivation.

2. Drinking 10 to 12 glasses of liquids daily. This increases your overall hydration level, and often increases the saliva in your mouth.
3. Breathing through your nose and not your mouth.
4. There are several over-the-counter sprays (Salivart, Roxane Saliva Substitute) that can keep the mouth and throat moist for several hours. They are nonsystemic solutions with no known side effects. Ask your pharmacist about them.

Harshness

This is the tense voice that is a common stress reaction for the person who "has had it." It usually occurs after exposure to prolonged, continuing stress. The voice sounds aggressive and is difficult to hear, the harsh voice can be replaced by the following suggestions:

1. Use the yawn-sigh. Practice speaking on the sigh. Here is no harshness in the sigh voice.
2. Practice keeping an open mouth while listening, reading, or watching TV, not agape, which could create a dry mouth, but with the lips slightly apart and with a relaxed jaw.
3. Dropping your pitch level one note will often make your voice sound softer.
4. Keep your head looking slightly down. Avoid extending the head upward. This helps relax the neck and throat muscles.
5. You might try neck relaxation by rolling your head in a circle. Start with your chin down. Roll your head to the left, then up and across to the right in a circle, and down and across. Continue rolling your head seven or eight times in one direction, then reverse directions.

High Pitch

A typical stress reaction is raised pitch. If you become aware that your pitch is consistently too high, go back to Chapter 7 and follow the procedures for both finding your natural pitch and lowering your pitch level. A high speaking pitch is usually the result of excessive vocal tract tension. Lowering your pitch can be helped by the following exercises:

1. Make a conscious effort to use a lower pitch. (This is often all you need to do.)
2. The yawn-sigh is a vocal tract relaxer and is helpful in lowering pitch.
3. Tilt your chin slightly down as you speak, and avoid extending the chin upward.
4. Make an effort to open your mouth more as you speak.

Hoarseness (Dysphonia)

Anyone who has had a normal voice and then suddenly becomes hoarse, yet doesn't have an allergy or a cold, can be displaying symptoms of a serious laryngeal disease. Anyone who is hoarse for more than seven days should have an ear-nose-throat examination. However, situational hoarseness that arises as a reaction to stress can be reduced by the following strategies:

1. Just trying to speak without hoarseness will sometimes eliminate it. Often with a little effort you can listen to yourself closely and eliminate your hoarseness.
2. Elevate your voice pitch one note.
3. Say fewer words per breath. Renew your breath by pausing more often when you speak (see Chapter 5).
4. Develop greater oral focus. Get your voice out of your throat (see Chapter 8).
5. At the end of a phrase or sentence, elevate your pitch.

Low Pitch

Some people speak at the very bottom of their pitch range as a reaction to stress. Speaking at such a low pitch usually reduces voice quality and makes your voice harder to hear and your speech more difficult to understand, particularly in noisy situations (which can cause stress to begin with). If your problem is low pitch under stress, the following exercises might be helpful:

1. Make a deliberate effort to speak a few notes above your bottom note.
2. Eliminate any throat voice focus you have. By developing good oral focus, so that your voice sounds as if it is coming off the surface of your tongue from the middle of your mouth, you will find it easier to achieve a higher pitch.

Monotone

Even people who most of the time have very spontaneous voices may develop a monotone under conditions of stress. A monotone lacks variations in both pitch and loudness. The rhythm and timing of speech sounds fixed and artificially steady. Becoming aware of a monotone is the first step for getting rid of it. Then making a conscious effort to vary pitch, loudness, and rhythm will often eliminate the monotone.

1. Practice some of the pitch inflection suggestions in Chapter 7.
2. Listen to a recording of your speech. Keep adding changes in inflection and volume until you don't hear the monotone anymore.

No Voice (Aphonia)

Total lack of voice can develop as a result of continued stress. This cannot be dealt with in a book such as this. Instead you should consult a speech-language pathologist or an ear-nose-throat doctor.

Pitch Breaks

Pitch breaks can be up or down. The voice usually breaks in the direction where it would like to be. If you are speaking too low, the voice breaks up, often an octave higher. If you are talking too high, the voice may break downward. When pitch breaks are a reaction to stress, they can often be wholly eliminated by changing your pitch level by one note. If your voice is breaking downward, lower your speaking pitch a note. For upward pitch breaks, raise your pitch a note. It should be pointed out that pitch breaks are a common phenomenon in young boys nearing the end of puberty. These pitch breaks are normal and usually disappear completely after three or four months without therapy.

Shortness of Breath

Sometimes people who usually have normal breathing become short of breath as a response to stress. They may have difficulty talking during these times, literally running out of air. If this is a problem of yours, and it is a very common one, try the following strategies.

1. Cut in half the number of words you try to say on one breath. Renew your breath more often by pausing more as you speak.
2. Try to speak louder. This may help your breathing.
3. Speak at a slightly higher pitch.

Strained Voice

Some people react to stress by developing a strained voice. The voice becomes tight, often high-pitched and harsh, and is difficult to hear and understand what is being said. Anything that can be done to relax the vocal tract will reduce voice strain.

1. The yawn-sigh approach is the most useful technique we have for reducing voice strain.
2. Avoid looking upward. When you speak, tilt your chin down slightly.
3. Practice simultaneously chewing and talking (see Chapter 11).
4. Develop a more open mouth (see Chapter 10).

Voice Breaks

Voice breaks are temporary loss of voice while speaking. For example, if someone wanted to say, "We are going to go on all the rides at Magic Mountain" with voice breaks, it would sound like: "We are going—to go on—all the rides—at Magic Mountain." Voice breaks can develop as a reaction to stress. When they do, the following things can be done to stop them:

1. It is most important to say fewer words per breath.
2. Vocal tract relaxation can help:
   • Use the yawn-sigh a bit.
   • Keep the head tilted down and minimize looking upward.
   • Keep your mouth slightly open and your teeth apart.
3. Soften the loudness of your voice.

Weak Voice

Sometimes continuous stress will result in a noticeable lack of voice volume. The weak voice often develops late among the reactions to stress symptoms. The voice sounds tired. It is low pitched with upward inflections at the end of phrases or sentences. The individual seems to be saying, "Will someone help me?" Help can come from practicing the following:

1. Say fewer words per breath and say them louder.
2. Get your voice focus out of your throat and put it up where it ought to be, on the surface of your tongue.
3. Elevate your voice pitch one note and inflect downward, instead of upward, at the end of sentences.

Remember, for any of these symptoms of stress in your voice, first do what you can to eliminate or reduce the stressors in your life. Once that is done, the exercises described in this chapter may help you find and maintain your natural voice in stressful situations.

CHAPTER 11

Stage Fright and Related Fears

*"I hoped my stage fright would vanish
when I began to give the speech."*

Stage fright is a term that describes a number of anxiety symptoms that many of us experience before speaking or performing in front of others. It is most troublesome if it still stays with us as we are performing. We know the physical symptoms well: excessive sweating of body or hands, cold hands, a flushed face, shaky knees, a need to go again to the bathroom, confusion, upset stomach, a tight feeling in the chest, and a dry mouth—and a change in our voices. There are many nonvocal performers, also, who may experience stage fright, such as a violinist before she plays a concerto or a golfer in a tournament who is about to make a putt.

Virtually any of the voice symptoms of stress listed in the last chapter can happen as part of stage fright, take a moment to review them. They will be familiar to any of you who have ever been "on-stage," making reports to fellow employees or supervisors, or speaking in meetings of all kinds, or even performing on a real stage for those of us who pursue acting or singing.

Stage fright is a special kind of stress reaction, and that is why we have devoted a separate chapter to it. For one thing, the reactions that we call stage fright commonly arrive in *anticipation* of a stressful situation. As we all know, stage fright gets its name from the experiences of performers preparing to go on stage. Commonly, they report that their stage fright is worse before the performance, rather than during it. In fact, most seasoned professionals quickly lose those butterflies in the stomach once they are on stage, but then they are professionals at performing, whereas most of us are not.

Another special thing about stage fright is that those preliminary signs of anxiety can show up no matter how many times one performs. Many other kinds of stress we can get used to, and our reactions will diminish. Not always so, it seems, with stage fright. The author can well remember his stage fright or preperformance anxiety while conducting a weekly series of television interviews. After interviewing particular guests before the television interview was to be taped, I can remember sitting on the set and feeling an urgent need for toileting and a strong desire to clear my throat. When the producer waved us "on" with the red light on the camera confirming that the taping was "live," these signs of preperformance anxiety went away. These performance jitters are well labeled as "stage fright."

Another characteristic of stage fright is the anxiety we feel when confronted by a challenge or opportunity. What causes the anxiety is fear of failing or not doing well. At the same time, we know that if we do well, we will be rewarded. Likewise, the stage performer hopes for applause, or even acclaim. Those of us who are onstage in other kinds of situations, if we perform well, are perceived as people who know what we are talking about, who can get things done and motivate others to work well with us or for us. Here are some other situations where we can suffer from stage fright.

Government Meetings

Many jobs today involve appearing before local, state, and federal government bodies. Your company wants to expand its plant? You may have to appear before government and zoning bodies to explain your firm's intentions, their impact on the environment, or why you need a zoning variance. Or your company may have learned of some ordinance or legislation that could adversely affect its business, and so you need to be heard by the city council, county supervisors, or state legislators—not all of these matters can be left to lawyers or professional lobbyists. As a resident of your community, a homeowner, or a parent, you may want to be heard by a planning commission, school board, community group, or even a city council or board of supervisors. Have you ever attended such meetings? Did you want to speak up on an issue of great concern to you? Did stage fright keep you quiet or make you present yourself poorly, or were you able to overcome it and speak well?

Professional Meetings

Thousands of associations and organizations have annual meetings where members present papers and participate in panel discussions. Do you volunteer to be part of these programs, or does stage fright hold you back? If you do speak, are you able to concentrate on what you are saying, or do you worry more about how you say it?

Business and Industry Meetings

Successful businesses today involve workers and management in a large number of meetings. You may be asked to give a report to your production team or sales staff, to review performance, and set goals and motivate people for the future. There are always meetings with clients or customers where you have to explain past performance, future goals, product innovations, and your superiority to competitors. There are also meetings with organized labor, lots of them when a contract is about to expire. Even if you are running your own small business, periodically you will need to gather your employees together for an informal meeting. The number of things that require meetings in today's business world seems endless, but they can be extremely important for you and your firm. During meetings, do you speak up? Are you able to say what you want to say? Are you relaxed, yet convincing when you speak?

Self-Help and Self-Study Groups

Many of us belong to self-help groups to help us in our careers, our social lives, or simply to broaden our interests. Did you ever notice how certain members of a group often dominate it because they speak more effectively? Do you have ideas, too, or questions you think need exploring? Does something always seem to hold you back? Do you remain silent because of a little stage fright?

Other Fear Situations

We can understand how fear can influence performance in athletics where speech and voice are not the problem. But what is the influence of fear on motor performance, such as when making a free-throw in basketball or sinking a long-distance putt in golf? You can probably think of many more situations where stress can influence performance. Perhaps the most common situation where many of us first experience stage fright, and continue to experience it, is in the job or promotion interview. There is a lot at stake at such times. And unfortunately, no matter how impressive your resume or performance record, or how sure you are that you can do this particular job better than anyone else, stage fright during the interview may cost you the opportunity. A poor voice can make you sound as if you are unsure of yourself, evasive or vague, or not the kind of person who can work effectively with others, or get them to work well with you.

Poise and presence are two qualities that are rated very highly in the business and professional world. By definition, stage fright deprives you of poise and presence.

Controlling Stage Fright and Other Fears

With most kinds of stress, we suggested that the first remedy to be considered is eliminating the stressor. We also said that in some cases this would be possible, and in others not. In the case of stage fright, very often, even most often, it is not desirable to eliminate the stress because what is causing it is a challenge or an opportunity.

What we must do then is control the symptoms of stage fright, learn to cope with the fear itself, and to control its impact on the voice. There are a couple of things about stage fright that make this easier to do than what you might expect. For one, remember that stage fright is largely an anticipatory fear; it hits us worst before we actually perform. This is a great advantage. Imagine if it worked the other way; that you had no fears at all before a speech, but they appeared when you stepped out in front of an audience. Because stage fright is largely an anticipatory fear, you have an opportunity to do something about the problem before you are actually on stage.

Another thing about anticipatory fear is that it "gets the adrenaline flowing." If we can learn to control the symptoms of fear, we can use our "pumped-up" condition to give a better performance. A little bit of well-managed stage fright can overcome apathy and give extra electricity to your manner and the way you speak. Any tiredness slips away.

Let us look now at ways to manage stage fright both before and during your performance. After that we will show you how to keep your natural voice at such times.

Six Ways to Control Stage Fright

Remember That Your Listeners Want You to Succeed

When you listen to people give a speech, or make a report of some kind, you are hopeful that what they say will be useful to you. Your listeners feel the same way about you. They want you to succeed. They will overlook many of your flaws, like a cracking voice or a little sweat on your brow, for the message you have to give. In fact, any of your signs of nervousness can be interpreted as flattering to your listeners, because they tell your listeners, in effect, "I am no better than you." Over my years in the classroom, I have noticed that students seem to feel more positively toward a speaker who shows some shyness rather than toward one who is glib and seemingly insensitive. So don't worry about showing a little nervousness.

Remember That We Hold Most Symptoms of Stage Fright Inside

Much nervousness is felt and not seen. In research projects at both the University of Denver and the University of Arizona, we looked at videotapes of ourselves in speech therapy and during supervisory conferences. Although we could not see signs of nervousness, such as change in heartbeat or warm blushing, as we watched ourselves on videotape, we relived and recalled the fears we had. Fortunately, most of these symptoms of fear could not be heard or seen by our listeners.

Look at the Audience Instead of Feeling You Are Being Looked At

There are two ways, one good and one bad, to stand before a group. The positive way is to look out and focus on the people in the audience. This helps you to forget yourself and focus instead on what you have to say. The bad way is to be aware of the audience looking at you. There is no surer way to encourage stage fright than too much self-focus before a group.

When I give a workshop or make a report at a meeting, I always pick out a few people who laugh or frown in reaction to what I say and do. I try to select people throughout the audience, so that my gaze moves around the room and is not limited to a seat or two. Wherever they sit, they must have reactive faces. They help me to focus out, not within. Also, if I observe a member of the audience who is sleeping or appears to be texting while I am presenting, or who portrays an opposite emotion from others in the audience, I immediately shift my attention away from this person. I focus instead on those who appear to be "with" me.

Reading a paper is a poor way to overcome stage fright. If the reader looks up from the printed text, he or she is liable to find that many in the audience are no longer paying attention. One of the joys of communication is relishing the reactions of your listeners. They are what you have worked so hard to get. So look out instead of within.

Concentrate on Your Message

An old actor told a drama class, "If you want to avoid stage fright, learn your lines!" The actor was saying to be prepared. As the speaker, you should know your topic better than most of your audience. Do not organize your presentation for those few "experts" in the audience. Prepare your remarks for the majority of people there. Prepare an outline for your presentation. Give yourself the freedom to speak from the outline rather than reading a text line by line. When we really know what we are talking about this is not hard, and we can enjoy our communication. Enjoying what we are doing is one of the best ways to avoid stage fright.

It is the spontaneous talk or report that gives many of us problems. We stand up at a meeting to state a position, or to respond spontaneously to another speaker. If we quickly get in over our heads, the symptoms of stage fright may hit us. There is nothing more destructive to clear thinking than a rush of stage fright. Even in spontaneous situations, we need to think before we speak. Don't be afraid to pause. A few moments of mental preparation can put your thoughts in order, and help you focus on what you say rather than how you are saying it. And your audience, too, will recognize a thoughtful pause for what it is, not as a sign of hesitancy or nervousness.

Replace Your Fear with Positive Thoughts

When Norman Vincent Peale wrote his classic *The Power of Positive Thinking*, he could just as well have titled the book, The Power of Negative Thinking. Negative thinking is as self-destructive as positive thinking can be self-fulfilling. A recent directory of the National Speakers Association shows that many of its members present lectures and workshops on self-confidence as the first step for increasing creativity and productivity. Positive thinking is also an important step for overcoming stage fright. Many of our stage fright fears are overreactions to previous situations in which we experienced symptoms of fear. You may have spoken up at a neighborhood association meeting and were unsure of yourself: Your face became flushed, your voice became tense, and you felt shaky in the knees. Since that experience, whenever you are in a group situation you fear that these symptoms will come back when you speak. That is the power of negative thinking. We generalize from an earlier unpleasant situation to a present situation.

And each speaking situation is a separate, unique opportunity. You may be speaking about different things. Your audience is different. And, most of all, you are different, because you are aware of that past experience and have learned from it. A big part of positive thinking is nothing more than having the confidence that you won't repeat your past mistakes. Learning the techniques to do that allow you to change negative thinking into positive thinking.

Replace Your Fears with Relaxation Techniques

Although stage fright and other fears appear to be universal conditions, keeping them in check seems to be a prominent characteristic of successful people. How many people have we known who have great speaking voices in private but are people almost struck dumb when they have to speak to a group? This is similar to a man who can play the violin like Joshua Bell, but only if no one is listening. The big difference between the amateur performer and the pro is that the professional has learned to stay relaxed. Performance success may be at least as much a matter of "keeping your cool" under pressure as it is a matter of talent and practice.

Here are four relaxation techniques that have proved helpful in the battle to diminish stage fright.

1. **The Relaxer.** Say, for example, you find yourself in a tense situation where you have to call someone on the phone with a very negative message. Before you make the call, sit in a chair with your arms hanging limp or in your lap. Drop your chin a little toward your chest, now close your eyes. Take in bigger, relaxed breaths. Inhale slowly through you nose, and then exhale the air through a slightly open mouth. Feel the openness of your airway. Picture in your mind that your mouth is slightly open, your tongue down, and your throat wide open. Don't think of anything else. Think only of your open mouth and throat. Keep your mouth open until your jaw and face seem somewhat heavy, a normal feeling when

you relax your mouth, jaw, and throat. Now, when you make that tough phone call you will find your stage symptoms have diminished.

2. **The Head Roll.** Keep your body in the same position you used with The Relaxer. With your mouth slightly open, roll your head slowly from side to side. Feel the heaviness of this movement. Now, practice rolling your head in a circular, clockwise pattern. From the chin-down position, with your mouth still open, roll your head to the left and then up so that you are looking at the ceiling. Continue across to the right and down and then across again. After eight clockwise rolls, reverse direction and roll your head counter-clockwise. The Head Roll is an excellent way to relax the head and neck, which often can tense up when you are anxious.

3. **The Invisible Yawn-Sigh.** This is an old professional's technique. Unlike the two previous exercises, which would be quite visible, the Invisible Yawn-Sigh can be done on the platform. It is simple to do once you practice it a few times. Keep your mouth closed and yawn (an exaggerated inspiration of air). Now let the air out with a closed-mouth sigh (the air exits through your nose). When you yawn-sigh like this it dilates and relaxes your throat. Experienced speakers and performers often use the Invisible Yawn-Sigh as they are being introduced on the platform or stage. Even if they are experiencing stage fright, when they speak after this exercise, their voice may sound perfectly relaxed.

4. **Progressive Relaxation.** One of the most effective relaxation techniques ever introduced was Jacobson's Progressive Relaxation. The technique begins by concentrating on a particular part of the body, such as the fingers or toes. Once you have isolated such a body part, say the toes, follow these steps:

   a. Lie on your back with your arms and legs extended. Close your eyes and concentrate on your toes for a few moments.

   b. Now curl your toes as hard as possible. Keep them contracted like this for 15 seconds. Then slowly relax them.

   c. Feel the sharp contrast between the tightness you experienced when the toes were contracted with the heaviness you feel when they are relaxed. Concentrate on this heavy feeling of relaxation.

At this point, you might then go on to the foot, the ankle, your hands. Some of you may have heard of these exercises as an aid in getting to sleep. They work. They also work well to get you in a physically and mentally relaxed state of mind before any situation that might cause stage fright.

Five Ways to Keep Your Natural Voice in Fear Situations

Although stage fright symptoms can be minimized by using the techniques just described, it is unlikely that any of us can completely eliminate them. Remember that many veteran performers, such as Jay Leno and former President George W. Bush, report that they still experience stage fright even after all their years of speaking before the camera and the public.

Remember, too, what we said earlier in this chapter: The stress that provokes these symptoms can be an asset because it can give our performances that little extra bit of electricity. That is only effective, however, when we are in control of the stage fright symptoms, and have not let them control us. Nowhere is that more important than with the voice.

Voice can, to use the old expression, "betray" your feelings of nervousness and anxiety. No matter how well your manner, expression, posture, and gestures conceal your anxiety, your voice can reveal your real state. Virtually none of the 12 voice symptoms of stress listed in the previous chapter are an asset when speaking. In fact, they all can have a very negative impact on your listeners.

Fortunately, there are a few techniques that will help you find and keep your natural voice despite feelings of fear. Some of the techniques you can only use before you go on stage—but that is when the symptoms of stage are often most acute. Others you can use during your performance, or just prior to speaking. Either way, by using one or several of the five techniques listed below, your voice can sound more natural and relaxed.

Develop an Open Mouth and Keep Your Teeth Apart

One of the bad things some people do when they have stage fright is to bite down hard on their molars and close their mouths. Many people even attempt to go on speaking through clenched teeth. The result is a voice that sounds strained and speech that is hard to understand. Or the frightened person sometimes bites down hard and grinds his molars together (known as *bruxism*), This also contributes to overall vocal tract tension, unintelligibility, and a very uncomfortable reaction from the audience.

When you experience stage fright, make a deliberate effort to keep your mouth slightly open. Keep your back molars slightly apart. Keep your lips slightly apart. Keep this slight opening between teeth and between lips, particularly when you are not talking. It will give you a relaxed feeling that will offset some of your tension.

The Chewing Method

This is another method that will help overcome the closed-mouth and clenched-teeth symptoms. It is particularly helpful for those who find this a persistent and severe problem. Look at yourself in a mirror or on your video as you count to 20. Do you open your mouth and move your lips and jaw as you speak? You should. The closed tight mouth, which can make you look like a ventriloquist, requires a lot of muscular effort, and can result in a voice that is unpleasantly tense and speech that is hard to understand.

If this is a problem for you, see if the six steps of the chewing method can help you.

1. Stand in front of a mirror and pretend that you are chewing three crackers at one time with an open mouth. Move your tongue around as if you were actually chewing. This exaggerated chewing (without food in your mouth) may not be attractive, but it is the first step in learning this technique. Your face will look a bit distorted, your jaw will move from side to side, and your mouth will be opened wider than usual. But this is only temporary.
2. Now add light voice, like a hum, to your exaggerated chewing. This will produce a monotonous "yum yum" sound. Do this briefly until you get the feeling of chewing simultaneously with voice. Now keep the chewing going, but instead of just humming say these two nonsense words: AHLAMETERAH and WANDAPANDA. Say them in a prolonged, chanting style, and chew them as you say them. Practice this until you feel relaxed doing it.

3. Now practice counting while you chew in this exaggerated manner. Slowly count: 1-2-3-4-5. This speaking while chewing (something our mothers told us not to do) is the start of developing normal mouth movements for speech.
4. Now practice reading a sentence or two while you chew.
5. Practice some spontaneous conversation as you chew. Watch yourself in a mirror or video playback. If you are comfortable with the exercise now, start to cut down the exaggerated mouth movements until the movements look normal. If you are concerned with what normal is, pay attention to what actors, actresses, and announcers do on television. What are their mouths doing as they speak?
6. In voice therapy, I usually end our practice chewing-speaking by telling my client, "From this point on when you speak, *think chewing.*" Just thinking about it will help you remember the feeling. We then combine the chewing method with the open mouth method we earlier discussed.

Keep Your Natural Pitch

There is a natural tendency for pitch to rise during anxious moments. In a fear situation, the larynx may rise in the neck and the laryngeal muscles may tighten. This contributes to the elevation of pitch. Not all people with stage fright experience this, but if you do the following steps should help.

Remember that in Chapter 7, we found that your natural pitch was usually two or three notes above the lowest note you could produce. If you find that your pitch rises during moments of stage fright, make a deliberate effort to bring it down to its natural level by following some of the pitch-lowering exercises in Chapter 7. In addition, the following tips might help you.

1. Keep your chin down and tilt your head toward your chest. It is easier to find a lower pitch with this head position.
2. Practice saying "uhm huh." Prolong the "huh" so it sounds like an "aaaaaaaah." Now sweep it down to near your lowest pitch. You should be able to go up a note or two from this level and be able to use that pitch level in fear or stress situations.

Renew Your Breath More Often

When we experience stage fright or other fears, our breathing sometimes becomes more irregular. If you feel that your breathing changes when you are fearful (many people do not experience this), there are a number of things you can do to correct it. Some of them you can do just before, others even during those times of stress.

1. Take a few deliberate long breaths. For example, as you are being introduced to speak, sit with your head slightly down and take in a long breath. Now let the air out slowly. Repeat several long breaths, in and out. It will give you much better control of your breathing.
2. Many people experience shortness of breath from stage fright, because they don't take in enough air with a breath OR because they try to say too many words on each breath. The best way to renew your breath while speaking is simply to pause. During the pause, your breath will renew itself with no special effort on your part. A wonderful example of using the pause to renew breath can be heard in Barack Obama's voice. He typically on television says five or six words per breath. He pauses and his breath automatically renews itself and he continues speaking. If you are experiencing stage fright, cut down the number of words you say on a breath. Pause. Then go on speaking. Pause again and then continue speaking.

Use the Yawn-Sigh

Stage fright can often close off your throat and make your voice sound tense and bottled up. As discussed earlier, the yawn-sigh is an excellent method for opening and relaxing the vocal tract. During the yawn, the pharynx is dilated. No matter how tight and closed off your throat may feel, if you yawn it will open up.

The procedures for doing the yawn-sigh are simple.

1. *Yawn.* Inhale with an open mouth. Really yawn, as you do when you are tired.

2. *Sigh*. Let the air out with a prolonged breathy sigh, tongue down, mouth open, throat open. There should be a light voice on the sigh.
3. *Extend the light-voiced sigh*. As you sigh, let your regular voice come out. This should be your natural voice. After the sigh, your voice should sound open, relaxed, and somewhat posterior in focus.

If you feel throat tightness build up as part of stage fright, use the yawn-sigh. This is a technique that you can use to relax your throat before you go on stage, but it can also be used just before speaking, or even during a pause when speaking, as we described a few pages back in The Invisible Yawn-Sigh. Either method will give you an open, back voice that is a much better voice than the high, tense voice we sometimes hear in someone with stage fright.

CHAPTER 12

Your Voice on Phones and Other Electronic Gadgetry

"After talking all day on the phone,
you could hear my voice getting tired."

In the past few years, there has been a barrage of new electronic equipment to use with our voices: landline phones at home and in the office, cellphones and smartphones used everywhere, tablets, portable TV cameras, amplifiers, and microphones. If we are not communicating with our voices, we are using our fingers for typing an endless number of text messages. This chapter is for the person of any age who uses his or her voice a lot while using these electronic devices.

None of these devices will make our voices sound good if we don't introduce a good voice to begin with. They are, after all, only mediums of transmission. The prime instrument of communication is still your own voice. The voice that we introduce through an instrument can be altered by treble and bass quality settings or distorted from inadequate or excessive amplification. We need to consider the various instrument categories separately to appreciate the different voice requirements needed for each instrument. The purpose of this chapter is to show you how to use your voice more effectively when using the instruments.

Telephones (Landline Phones)

Although most social conversations are now using the cellphone and the smartphone, the cordless land phone is a mainstay in many homes and an absolute must in most offices. How well we use the land phone varies greatly from person to person. Some people are "good on the phone," others are not. Some people like talking on the phone; others, even over a lifetime, dislike it and it shows in their voices. Some people feel uncomfortable "on stage" on the telephone while others use it casually and easily. Some people yell unnecessarily on the phone, as if they have to project their voices by talking louder. One coworker of mine was heard to use a louder voice only for long distance calls, as if the miles between him and his distant listener required the need for talking louder. Remember that the phone is a voice amplifier. Therefore, the best land phone voice is the Number Two, Soft Voice, we talked about in Chapter 6, Loud Enough or Too Loud?

The telephone is only a voice transmitter, not a voice enhancer. If you habitually use a poor voice, and do nothing to improve it, you will have a poor voice on the phone. About the only people whose speaking voices can be improved on the phone are those who normally speak too softly.

The only way the phone transmits our communication is by the sound of our voice. Yet, we have all known people who are just as animated in gestures and body language in phone conversations as they are in face-to-face conversations. That is all very well if those feelings can show in their voices, too. Often they do not. Such people are always surprised or upset when their phone messages are misunderstood, when the listener cannot see to react to their visual gestures or expressions.

A few simple techniques can help you to present yourself as you really are, effectively convey what you mean and feel, and put you as much at ease on the telephone as you are in personal conversation. Let us look at these techniques by examining the most common problems people encounter in using the landline phone.

Voice Identity on the Phone

Despite *Caller ID,* which identifies the caller before you pick up the phone, identifying who you are is the first requisite in making a call. People who are apprehensive or uncomfortable using a phone frequently are convinced that the person they have called will not know who they are, even if that person knows them fairly well. Other people make phone calls with utter confidence that they will be instantly identified, which can be a real problem for the listener.

We have all had calls from both types. The first person usually gives his first name right away and often, after an uncertain pause, his last name and other identification, such as "Hello. This is Randy. Randy Brown. Randy Brown from Mason Industries." If the person getting the call already knows the caller reasonably well, such an opening sounds unnecessary. The second type of caller usually doesn't give his name or, if he does, gives only a first name, "Hi. This is George. Where is the shipment you invoiced us for last Thursday?" This approach can also have a negative result, particularly if the person calling is not that well known, or if the person receiving the call deals with large numbers of people on the phone, several of whom might be named George.

The point is that identification of the caller is of major importance in phone communication. In fact, those who are apprehensive or uncomfortable on the phone take note—the best thing you have going for you when you phone someone is that you are making the call. The person answering hopefully recognizes you, whom you represent, and about what you may be calling. This quick orientation makes it possible for the conversation to go smoothly. But even when you give your name at the beginning, as you should, it is important that you continue to sound like yourself. You will also need to avoid some of the following problems.

Loudness Problems on the Phone

The two most common difficulties in phone conversations are speaking too softly or speaking too loudly. Although the phone is an amplifier and many soft-spoken people get a needed loudness boost, others make needed amplification impossible by holding the phone too far away from their mouths, or turning their faces away from the instrument.

On the other hand, the land phone's power can be a disadvantage for the person who speaks too loudly, or holds the transmitter too close to the mouth. The result can be voice distortion. Not only does this make it difficult for conversation, but the person called can be as irritated by a loud, distorted voice as by a voice that is too soft to hear. People with loudness problems using the phone should remember that the instrument is designed for the adult-sized head. When the receiver is at your ear, the transmitter end of the phone should extend down below your mouth, a few inches away from your chin.

The best loudness level on the land phone is a light voice. Remember back in Chapter 6 when we talked about the Level 2 voice, a voice loud enough to be heard but not so loud that it would awaken someone sleeping nearby? This is the best landline phone loudness level. The Level 3, conversational voice, is often too loud. We never hear what our normal voice sounds like to the listener on the other end of the line. Only on those rare occasions when we listen to ourselves on an answering machine can we appreciate the different voice quality we hear on the phone versus the voice we hear "live" as we speak.

If you listen to your voice on an answering machine, how does your voice loudness compare to other people's messages you have received? If you don't have an answering machine, ask a friend or family member to rate your loudness. After such tests, all you really need to do is stay aware of the position of the transmitter relative to your mouth, use a Level 2 voice volume, and maintain your natural pitch a couple of notes above the lowest note you can produce.

The Tense Voice

If a tense voice is your problem, before you answer the phone or make a call, open your mouth and take in and let out a few big breaths. This will also give you time to think about what you want to say. Then our old friend the yawn-sigh is often helpful for maintaining a relaxed phone voice—and on the phone you don't have to worry about the yawn being seen. It will also help if you remember to renew your breath by pausing now and then as you speak.

The Unfriendly Voice

Although there are times when an unfriendly voice on the phone is called for (as when you're asking someone to pay a bill for the umpteenth time), usually a friendly voice is a better way to get things done. Unfortunately, some of us frequently sound unfriendly on the phone, often without meaning to. This can be just a matter of not paying attention to what we are doing. After all, most phone calls arrive unexpectedly. We may be concentrating on something or on someone else, and when we pick up the phone, we don't make an adjustment in our mood or voice, or we may be a little irritated at the interruption.

To gain some control over whether you sound friendly or unfriendly on the phone, try this simple experiment. Use your answering machine, or ask a friend or relative to help. When you speak on the phone deliberately smile as you speak. Then deliberately frown. It is virtually impossible to do both at the same time. Now listen to the recording of your voice, or ask a friend or relative if those changes in expression were heard in your voice. Research has found that there is a significant acoustic difference between a smiling and a frowning voice. If it is to your advantage to sound friendly on the phone, speaking with a smile can help. You can prepare for it by thinking about something pleasant. It also helps to remember that, just as it is important to you to be recognized on the phone, recognition is important to others too. When you visualize the person on the other end of the line, a more personal feeling should be heard in your voice.

The Unconcerned Voice

This might be termed passive unfriendliness. The person using this voice sounds cold or impersonal. You may have noticed that even some of the people you know well speak this way on the phone. They sound as if they are talking to a stranger, and you want to say, "Wait a minute. This is me." Or we make or receive a call from a call center. Here we push a series of numbers in our search to talk to a "live" person. Or we call a company and are told to hold for someone to help us. After a few minutes waiting, we may hear the message, "Please hold for the next available agent as your call is very important to us." The person finally answering the call may have an artificial friendliness, and we have to work hard to keep our annoyance from sounding in our voices.

Or the unfriendly voice often belongs to a person who feels that a conversation with a person they can't see, and who can't see them, isn't a real conversation at all. But it is also common among people who are overworked, harassed, or who have to spend a great deal of time on the phone. What comes through is that they are just making, or receiving "another call," rather than talking to an individual.

The best corrective action, particularly when you have been having a hectic day, is to take a moment before you make a call or answer the phone to visualize the person you are going to speak with, and accommodate your voice for that person. You can reinforce this personalization by using the other person's name with some frequency in the conversation, instead of just delivering your message. This is also the time for you to deliberately improve your mood before a call, and use the smile when you are talking. A friendly voice is never an unconcerned voice.

The Scared Voice

It seems strange in this technological age, but there are some people who are frightened using the landline phone, but are comfortable using their cell phones. They are nervous when the phone rings. They make calls reluctantly. Before they punch out the numbers, they may rehearse what they plan to say or clear their throats. When they speak they sometimes seem to be "trying on" different voices, looking for the right one to use. In short, the frightened person sounds nervous, uncertain, and uncomfortable. If they are usually frightened meeting new people, then the problem is not in the phone. But if they generally relate well to people but have a problem doing so on the phone, then the phone has become the primary obstacle to communication.

Here are a few ways to desensitize such a "phone phobia." First, remember that the telephone is just a plastic, lifeless electronic instrument designed to convey your voice messages to someone who is not near you. The phone's sole purpose is to make communication possible for you, not harder.

Second, practice speaking on the phone by turning it off or unplugging it but pretending you are talking on a "live" phone. Practice speaking or reading aloud on the disconnected instrument until you feel more comfortable doing so.

Third, reconnect the telephone and call either your answering machine or a friend, relative, or family member. Try to maintain the ease that you achieved when you spoke into the same phone when it was turned off.

As in some of the previous problems we have discussed, another way to overcome "phone phobia" is to visualize the person you are calling, or who has called you, and to personalize the conversation by using the person's name. Often this will cause the other person to use your name more frequently, which will put you more at ease, too.

Finally, for those of you with a serious case of "phone phobia," review Chapter 11, Stage Fright and Related Fears. The same relaxation techniques that work before a live audience will help you with that electronic device called a telephone.

Cellphones and Smartphones

In the middle 1990s, we began to see the emergence of the cellphone. It had wireless capability, which gave it portability to be used almost anywhere. It was downsized to fit easily in the palm of an adult hand. And the first cellphones allowed one to make and receive phone calls in nearly all settings. By the end of the 1990s, the cellphone flourished everywhere. The cellphone was particularly attractive to youth, who to this day can be observed on most campuses holding their cellphones to their ears and having continuous conversations with their peers. From a voice point of view (the focus of this book), some people complain of vocal fatigue. In most cases, the tired voice recovers from not talking during the sleeping hours. Upon awakening, the voice sounds normal, only to begin tiring again after a day of prolonged talking. Sometimes a heavy user of cellphones may develop a more permanent hoarseness, requiring voice therapy provided by a speech-language pathologist.

The cellphone of the late '90s added personal digital assistants (PDAs), which were tied into one's computer. The PDA was able to store information, which came in through the cellphone and could create things like a "to-do" list, which could be stored on your computer.

Eventually, the cellphone with its PDAs was able to send and receive email, serve as a camera, a TV cam, and playback. It can now do so many things it is now rightfully called a "smartphone." The smartphone today has capability of running innumerable applications (Apps). The App menus are continually changing but through the App stores we can find many programs we can use in voice: amplifiers, auditory feedback devices, programs for measuring voice pitch and voice loudness (intensity) measure. Although there has been some increase in size of some smartphones, the majority of them are still palm-sized, which allows their continuous use as a telephone. The voice usage and voice problems that may arise from continuous heavy use are the same we mentioned above for cellphones

The Microphone

Mike fright is a term that originated in the early days of radio, and refers to the same kinds of symptoms that we read about as stage fright. For many people, the sight of a microphone is enough to make them panic. A whole movie, *The King's Speech*, depicted Britain's King George VI's fear of the microphone in his attempts to overcome his stuttering. Yet a microphone used well can enhance one's voice and greatly facilitate communication between a speaker and an audience. Also, before sizable groups and in large rooms, a microphone is necessary for effective communication.

A good public address (PA) system, consisting of microphone, amplifier, and speakers, has far greater audio fidelity than a telephone. It can pick up all the high and low pitches of your voice, its resonance, and even compensate to some extent for lack of voice focus. Some people with ineffective, or unremarkable, voices in person can sound much better over a PA system.

However, this is true only if he or she knows how to use it properly. Most of us have had little or no experience using a microphone, and if used poorly, it can make a shambles out of what you are trying to say.

Make sure the amplifier settings are right for you. The typical amplifier has controls for setting volume (also called gain) and bass and treble. You want to get these right for your voice before the audience arrives. A little more bass will give you a deeper, more resonant sound if you need it. More treble will help your voice carry better. Most of our consonants are high-frequency sounds, so setting the treble higher will emphasize them and make you easier to understand by people with some hearing loss.

There are several types of microphones in use today. The most common type is a cordless mike mounted on a floor stand or a table or podium stand. It can usually be detached from the stand so the speaker can hold the mike in his hand and move freely around the stage or platform. Whether it remains on the stand or is held in the hand, the person speaking must be constantly aware of the distance between his or her mouth and the microphone. With a sensitive microphone, even small variations in that distance can make a large difference in sound.

Watch the distance between your mouth and the microphone. This is important for those using a microphone on a floor stand, or mounted on a lectern or a hand-held mike. It is best to keep the microphone at chin level rather than mouth level. This will prevent that occasional explosive sound that occurs if you get a little too close, and it also keeps the audience from hearing you take in a breath. Although there is no one distance from the microphone mounted on a stand that is best for everyone or every situation, our personal experience is the preferred mike placement is somewhere between six and twelve inches from our chin.

Fortunately today, speakers, teachers, and workshop presenters have the choice of using either a lavaliere mike hung around the neck or a clip-on type that is clipped to one's clothing. Both of these two mike choices offer the speaker no variation in mouth-to-mike difference.

Once you have made yourself familiar with the public address equipment, you can and should forget about it. The impression you want to convey to your audience is that you are speaking to them, not your voice coming out of the loudspeakers. So always look beyond the microphone at your audience. As far as you and they are concerned, the mike is not there.

It is important to control the emotions in your microphone voice. In our chapters on stress and stage fright we gave suggestions for controlling the symptoms of fear and stress in your voice. These are particularly important when you talk on a microphone because the device can markedly amplify emotion in your voice. A fear-induced tremor or a hint of strain that might go unnoticed in ordinary conversation can be reproduced with excruciating fidelity over a good PA system. The system's amplification can also be a problem because many of us in situations of stress may speak much louder than normal. Many a nervous speaker has startled an audience out of their seats by his booming words. Changes in pitch are also common symptoms of stage fright and stress that can be exaggerated by a PA system.

If you are one of those people who get "mike fright," or if you are simply inexperienced in using a PA system, it would be a good idea to have the suggestions in Chapters 10 and 11 firmly in mind before you find yourself with a microphone between you and your audience.

Voice Amplifiers

There are many portable voice amplifiers available that can be of use to teachers, coaches, narrators, and tour guides. Sometimes a professional with a "tired" voice finds a voice amplifier to be a voice-saving instrument after prolonged speaking. Most voice amplifiers can be worn around the waist or clipped to belts or jackets. This type has the amplifier and speaker together in one portable unit with an attached lavaliere or clip-on microphone. A second type of voice amplifier is really a miniature and personal PA system. The voice amplifier has fixed speakers set in various parts of the room with the teacher or narrator speaking through a lavaliere or clip-on mike.

Although both types of mikes have fixed mouth-to-mike distances, the body-worn mike is perhaps more sensitive for causing distortion. A common mistake when using a body-worn amplifier is speaking too loudly into the microphone. We see our audience around us, and our attempts to reach out to them often result in our using a louder voice too close to the mike. This distorts the voice and can produce unwanted speaker noise or squeals.

A generalized recommendation for using a voice amplifier is to use your natural voice (as discussed in previous chapters) at a moderate loudness level. One must let the amplifier produce the loudness needed and not use a moderate or loud voice to do it. There are innumerable voice amplifiers on the market, and the "for sale" listings are continually changing. Our purchase recommendation is to stay away from the low-price units, and consider your selection from just above the mid-price level toward the high-end cost listings.

CHAPTER 13

The Female Voice

*"After talking at work all day, my voice
sounds hoarse before I go home."*

In this chapter, we take a look at the female voice before puberty through old age. We consider the physical factors, primarily hormonal, that heavily influence the sound of the female voice. We then look at some of the social factors in modern society that shape the way women sound. And, finally, we offer specific suggestions for correcting some voice problems, which can help most women find and maintain their natural voices in the various situations in which they find themselves: at work, home, and play.

The Female Voice

We all know that an adult female voice is higher in pitch than an adult male voice at the same age. What we often do not appreciate, however, is that the female voice pitch also drops markedly as girls go through puberty. At age 9, most boys and girls have the same voice pitch (around 265 Hz or slightly above middle C on the musical scale). During puberty, the female speaking voice drops three or four musical notes. By age 20, a common pitch level for young adult women is an A below middle C (near 220 Hz). As we see in Figure 13–1, the adult female voice pitch generally lowers slightly over the life span. (For further details

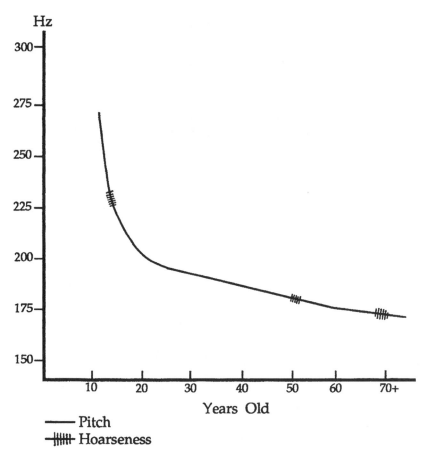

Figure 13–1. Female voice changes over time.

about pitch changes, you wish to look again at Figure 7–1 and to review the early sections of Chapter 7, The Well-Aimed Pitch.)

As women grow older, their pitch level gets lower. Their voices also get rougher at times, as you can see by the cross-hatches on the pitch line in Figure 13–1. This vocal roughness, we generally call hoarseness. Some girls experience mild hoarseness during their early teenage years. If they were also high school cheerleaders, they may experience more hoarseness caused by their forced yelling. This vocal roughness will usually disappear during their 20s, 30s, and 40s giving the typical woman a clear, normal voice during the majority of her working years.

After menopause, women typically experience some lowering of pitch, sometimes accompanied by a small amount of hoarseness with each new decade of life. Fortunately, research studies in recent years suggest that older women who are physically fit seem to display the same clarity of voice as younger women.

Another prominent voice characteristic of the American woman is that her voice pitch has a tendency to inflect upward toward the end of a sentence. This is in contrast to the typical male voice pattern, which characteristically drops downward at the end of a sentence. This upward inflectional shift appears to be culturally learned and often projects an image of a more passive person. The more aggressive, classic male voice inflects down, conveying an image of confidence.

Unlike pitch and hoarseness characteristics that are more physical in origin, voice inflection behavior appears to be learned, and generally follows the stereotypic model that one perceives as fitting for one's age, sex, and role. As we will see later in this chapter, voice patterns can be changed to meet the self-image requirements of any particular situation. For example, a woman who is continually interrupted as she is speaking by another person (usually male) might be advised to use more downward inflections at the end of sentences.

Physical Voice Changes in the Female

In this section, we will look at physical changes that influence the voice of the normal woman. We will not consider vocal abnormalities and their causes, which have been mentioned in other chapters.

The human larynx is heavily influenced by hormonal changes. The female in particular seems to experience hormone-induced voice changes during particular times in her life, such as during puberty, menstruation, pregnancy, and the menopause.

The pubescent changes in the female larynx are well documented. With the increase of estrogen (female hormone), the cartilages and muscles of the larynx enlarge greatly in size. The vocal folds of a 10-year-old girl are about 10-mm long; by age 15, they have increased to the adult length of 14 to 17 mm. These changes in size contribute to the lowering of the girl's natural speaking voice. As you may remember from earlier chapters, voice pitch is directly related to the tension and size (length and thickness) of the vocal folds. A young woman may also experience a small amount of hoarseness as part of her menstrual cycle related to a slight swelling of the membranes covering her vocal folds.

Although much has been written about the irritability, depression, fatigue, bloating, weight gain, and possible breast pain that can be part of the premenstrual syndrome, only in recent years have changes of voice been documented. Dr. Jean Abitbol and other physicians in Paris studied 38 female professional voice users between the ages of 21 and 40. He found that 22 of them experienced premenstrual symptoms of hoarseness and vocal fatigue. Most of them experienced no voice difficulties later in the ovulation stage of their menstrual cycle.

Many investigators have found that the female vocal folds at the premenstrual time are often swollen with some water retention and vascular enlargement. Dr. Chen (personal communication) at the Shanghai Conservatory in China studied 69 female opera singers and found that 86% of them experienced premenstrual vocal symptoms related to vocal fold swelling. She reported that this enlargement resulted in a slight lowering of voice pitch that was often accompanied by slight hoarseness.

These voice complaints are not anxiety-induced or psychogenic in origin; they are caused by physical changes of the vocal folds. For example, the loss of a note or two at the top of the singing range is well documented for female opera singers at premenstrual times. Consequently, most major opera companies today have "grace days" built into their singers' contracts. A few days before their periods, female vocalists do not sing.

During the premenstrual period, women who use their voices a lot in their work should make a special effort to cut down vocal effort and try to use voice in as easy a manner as possible. Many of the suggestions in Chapter 15, Ten Steps for Keeping Your Natural Voice, will be helpful. From age 20 through the late 40s, the voice of the normal woman holds up very well. There is a slight lowering of pitch over time, as we saw in Figure 13–1. Other than the mild vocal symptoms she may experience during a few premenstrual days, her voice is basically trouble free. If she is a heavy smoker or suffers from a severe respiratory disease, she will possibly experience voice problems that interfere with normal voice.

Despite the hormonal shifts experienced during most of pregnancy, effects on voice seem to be minor. From the seventh month on, however, the pregnant woman may find that the growing baby inside her interferes a bit with normal breathing. She might need to renew her breath more often by saying fewer words per breath.

Perhaps the biggest hormonal influence on the female voice comes during and after the menopause. Less estrogen is available, while at the same time there is some increase in the male hormone (testosterone), causing increased thickness of the membranes covering the vocal folds. The postmenopausal woman also carries her larynx a bit lower in the neck. All of these physical changes seem to contribute to a continued lowering of pitch level in advancing age. The hoarseness that some older women may experience seems to occur more often in women who show other sensory/motor changes related to aging. Older women in good physical shape are less likely to show any voice hoarseness.

The typical older female free of any laryngeal disease will probably have a normal, if lower, speaking voice. If she experiences a voice problem, some of the suggestions given later in this chapter for women of all ages may be of some help.

Of some interest is the common finding that the speed of speaking goes down with increasing age in both men and women. It takes older people longer to say the same passage than it does younger people. This slowing is perhaps directly caused by diminished breathing functions, such as lower lung volumes and reduced air pressures. This requires the older person to renew breath more often. Also, older people tend to prolong the vowels in the words they say (for reasons we do not know). Thus, reduced breath support and vowel prolongation probably contribute to fewer words said per minute in both older men and women.

The Social Aspects of Women's Voices

The American woman has made tremendous economic and social gains in the past 40 years. For the most part, her speaking voice has served her well as she has taken on professional and administrative responsibilities that previously belonged to males in such diverse fields as industry, banking, transportation, medicine, or law.

The majority of working women are married and have children. Unlike the husband, whose primary focus in life is more often his work, the typical female makes definitive role changes from her role in the workplace to her roles of wife and mother. These role shifts are often accompanied by changes in voice, and here is where some vocal difficulties can occur.

In the voice clinic, we recently saw a 31-year-old sales executive, Lori, who was experiencing hoarseness and pain in her throat that appeared to be related to stress. Her day began early in the morning when she got breakfast for her lawyer husband and two children, ages 2 and 4. No one spoke much at that time, and when Lori spoke it was usually to hurry the children along so she could leave them at a day care center and still make it to her office by eight o'clock.

As the chief executive of a 22-person office and sales staff, she used her voice all day long. She often used what she considered "a voice of authority," which was lower in pitch and much louder than the voice she used at home. On the office telephone, she used a gentler voice, only to return to the authoritarian voice with the next office appointment. By the nature of her work, her days were filled with tension, and this tension caused her to clear her throat a lot.

In the evening, her husband picked up the children, and they were usually home before Lori got there. Lori and her husband prepared dinner together while the children played in the playroom next to the kitchen. During dinner, and until the children went to bed, Lori spent much time disciplining the children, often with a high-pitched censuring voice. Finally, after the children were asleep, Lori and her husband had some time together, during which she spoke in an easy, natural voice.

The story of Lori could be replicated by many young mothers. She was caught in three distinct roles: executive, mother, and wife. She had learned to use a different voice in each role. The best thing we were able to do for Lori's voice problem was to show her ways to use her natural voice in all situations. This helped her greatly. Because of the constantly changing vocal demands that women face, some women like Lori, who change vocal roles often during a day, can develop hoarseness, pain in the throat, loss of voice volume, vocal fatigue, and sometimes complete loss of voice.

A good speaker, male or female, makes it look easy. Normal voice takes a minimum of effort. We have all heard women's voices that seemed to be produced with little or no effort. They are pleasant voices and are easy to listen to, perhaps similar to these four famous voices:

- *Hillary Clinton.* Despite her intensive travel and continuing stressful situations, she always seems to speak with a normal voice, appropriate in quality and loudness.
- *Madonna.* Although she produces many vocal excesses as she sings, her speaking voice usually shows good, clear quality.
- *Meryl Streep.* No matter what accent she may be using or what role she is playing, she always keeps a clear voice with excellent voice focus.
- *Betty White.* This veteran television actress in her late 90s keeps a clear, youthful sounding voice. Also, she has a friendly voice to hear.

Some women's voices are less pleasant than those mentioned above. Usually they are produced with too much effort. Once again if we look at the voices of some well-known women in the past and present, we can find some examples. Their problem voices are part of their distinctive personalities:

- *Bette Davis.* We remember this wonderful actress for her changing and interesting voice. Her hoarseness with her abrupt way of speaking became her trademark.
- *Julia Child.* The distinctive voice of this culinary commentator was characterized by high-pitched voice breaks. Her distinctive voice became better known than what she had to say.

In many radio-TV markets, we hear the hypernasal shrill voices of young women reading the news or on commercials. Such unpleasant voices could be softened.

There are good and bad voices all around us. If we develop an awareness of them, we can set better goals for our own voices.

Common Problems of the Female Voice

As we will see in the last section of this chapter, searching for and maintaining one's natural voice is the key to avoiding voice problems. The voice of a woman (like the voice of anyone) should mirror how she really feels inside. Because our inner feelings are always changing, the normal voice is always changing. Some voice change for different situations is to be expected.

The voice becomes a problem when the sound of the voice and the way it is produced interfere with communication. The way you sound may be telling your listeners something different than the words you are saying. You may sound angry when inside you do not feel that way. Or your voice may sound as if you are unsure of yourself while inside you are fully confident of what you are doing. And sometimes we may need a different voice to hide our real feelings from our listeners. We don't want our listeners to know by the sound of our voice that we may be angry or afraid or inappropriately happy. Let us look at some voice styles that carry particular images to our listeners.

Excessive Use of Low Pitch

Many women think it is attractive to use the lowest speaking pitch they can produce. Some feel this carries an authoritative sound that helps them sound as if they are in control of a situation. Some women think there are advantages to sounding like men, often not realizing that their natural voices may give them better control of some situations. Some women think that imitating the low-pitched voice of someone like former actress Lauren Bacall presents them as sexy and seductive. Interestingly, such low-pitched voices are not heard often by younger women under the age of 30.

There is probably no voice behavior harder on the larynx than speaking at too low a pitch. Speaking at the bottom of one's pitch range seems to cause the voice to lose its natural resonance. It sounds strained. It is difficult to hear. And over time, the excessively low-pitched voice can lead to vocal fold pathology.

Using Hard Glottal Attack

As described in earlier chapters, hard glottal attack is speaking with exact precision, with each word sounding separated from other words. Such a voice replaces the normal speaking legato with a crisp staccato. Each word seems to require separate voicing. The former actress Bette Davis' voice was a classic example of abrupt glottal attack. Some female administrators use hard glottal attack to control the people around them.

Such a voice is hard to listen to over time. The woman who uses such a crisp attack is signaling her listeners: "I know what I'm talking about—don't you dare challenge me!" Obviously, such a speaking style is viewed as aggressive by many listeners. Such precise speech also makes listening difficult. Over time, this crisp speaking style can lead to tissue changes (contact ulcers) on the back part of the vocal folds.

Using Heavy Word Stress

Far more female than male radio-television newscasters use exaggerated word stress. By word stress we mean saying a syllable or a word in a higher pitch, or a bit louder, and often stretching out the word (prolonging the vowels). In listening to a recording of a female newscaster commenting on an abortion ruling by the Supreme Court, I heard these words stressed (in caps):

> It is TIME for the women of AMERica, the PRIMary consumers in this NATion, to STAND UP for what IS their BAsic right.

Such continuous word stress defeats the purpose of using such stress, which is to highlight an occasional word within the sentence. It is hard on one's listeners, yet it is commonly used by broadcasters on local and national radio and television. In everyday life, we do not hear too many women speak this way. When we do, they are usually in some kind of leadership role where the use of word stress may be equated in their minds with aggressiveness and authority.

Speaking Too Softly

Some women complain that they are often not heard, particularly by their male coworkers. This is particularly common among women whose voices are low-pitched with an obvious focus in their throats. Other women continue to use the same voice loudness, whether they are speaking to one person or to a group of people. The person who speaks too softly is often viewed by listeners as shy, timid, and perhaps feeling inferior. Just by speaking louder, these perceptions can change quite favorably for the speaker.

Voice Tips for the Female Adult

There is a diversity of roles for women today, and each perhaps requires some individualization of voice style. Some women love the role of being single, with all of the opportunities and restrictions that such a life brings. Others prefer the traditional role of homemaker and mother. Many women combine the roles of worker, mother, and wife. Others, as single parents, work to support their children. Some women prefer the challenge of executive and professional work situations, making their careers the primary focus of their lives. Obviously, for the female adult, there is no one voice for everyone and for every role situation. Certainly there will be situations where some special use of voice is needed. For example, there may be times when you are unsure of a solution to a problem but it is important that you mask this unsureness from the people around you. There may be a need to hide fear or uncertainty.

It does appear, however, that over the long haul most women will experience the best voice by trying to keep their natural voices, regardless of the situation in which they find themselves. The earlier chapters in this book that talked about respiration, loudness, pitch, focus, and nasality have relevance for every woman seeking to find and improve her natural voice. The tips below will help you develop voice control in particular situations.

Keep Your Pitch Where It Ought to Be

Throughout this book, we have talked about using a speaking pitch that is a few notes above your lowest pitch. Avoid speaking too low or too high. A 38-year-old female surgeon, Dr. B, began using the lowest-pitched voice she could produce during her afternoon office hours. Apparently during her morning surgery schedule, she used a natural voice and experienced no problems. But by using her low-pitched voice all afternoon, by five o'clock Dr. B's voice was reduced to a whisper. Speaking very long at the bottom of your pitch range can play havoc with the voice.

Don't be afraid to use a lower voice now and then to fit a particular situation, but don't make the mistake of using this low pitch all the time. Authority can be added to your voice just by dropping your voice pitch toward the end of a phrase or sentence. Most of the time, keep your pitch up where it ought to be. And remember, avoid speaking in a monotone by developing good pitch variability.

Keep a Good Voice Focus

Maintain the imagery of placing your voice right off the surface of your tongue in the center of your mouth. This will avoid the "eensy weensy" baby voice that comes from having the tongue too far forward. It will also avoid the "country bumpkin" voice caused from back tongue carriage. Most importantly, it will keep the focus of your voice out of your throat.

A voice with good oral focus signals a healthy voice. There are very few hoarse voices with good oral focus. A focused voice will last all day, despite various vocal demands placed on it. It will produce a voice that people around you find easy to hear.

Change Your Loudness to Fit the Situation

There is no voice more boring than one that always uses the same pitch and loudness. At home with a child or a husband is an excellent place to play with the loudness of your voice. Like the whisper, save the moderately loud voice for certain situations. Whenever possible, avoid shouting (substitute a whistle or a bell instead of yelling at the kids).

In the work setting, it is important to vary the loudness of your voice for certain situations. Alicia, who was a telephone receptionist, sounded fine on the phone but used the same loudness level with people who stopped at her desk. No one could hear her. Noisy occupations, such as working as an airline cabin attendant or on an assembly line, require one to speak in a louder voice to overcome the constant background noise. Women, like men, have a loudness control to speak softer or louder. Use it.

Use More Downward Pitch Inflections

The upward pitch inflection at the end of a sentence denotes a question or unsureness. The voice of authority is usually characterized by a dropping inflection at the end of a sentence. As mentioned earlier in this chapter, women in most cultures tend to use more rising inflections than men do. This may be why, according to recent communication research, men may "one-up" what women say, and often interrupt them. The rising inflection may be a signal for the man (or the other person) to interrupt and begin speaking.

In any case, become aware of the power of inflections at the end of sentences. For the woman who wants more command in her voice, dropping her voice a note or two toward the end of the sentence will usually give her voice more authority.

Change Your Glottal Attack to Fit the Situation

Similar to pitch and loudness changes, occasional use of hard glottal attack can give more emphasis to what you are saying. But hard glottal attack should be reserved for those few situations where you need to make a point. Avoid sounding like some male or female television newscasters who use hard glottal attack for almost every word they say. Continuous use of hard glottal attack gives unneeded emphasis and can be very irritating to listeners.

Use a soft-voice attack (like Southern speech) now and then. This easy legato and soft glottal attack sounds as if it takes very little effort. It's easy to listen to. Use soft attack during easy, relaxed moments and feel how relaxing it can be to speak this way. The actress Joanne Woodward, whose early years were spent in Mississippi, still shows traces of easy glottal attack and is a good model for older women to use such an effective, easy voice.

Use Word Stress for Occasional Emphasis

Word stress is giving particular words or syllables more voicing emphasis. Stressed words and syllables can be higher in pitch, louder, and/or more prolonged than normal. For women who are in a position of authority, occasional use of word stress can be very useful. But save word stress for the few words that are truly important. Excessive use of word stress can work against you, often making you sound too aggressive and too self-important. Avoid sounding like some broadcasters we mentioned earlier who stressed every third word or syllable. Such speech can become meaningless, as well as irritating to listeners.

Finding a Few Voice Models to Emulate (and to Stay Away From)

Most of us have people whom we admire—athletes, actresses, politicians, your sister, or the woman next door. Make a list of people whose voices you like to hear and of those whose voices you do not like to hear. I made up lists of good and poor voices in the last section. Picking a voice model is a highly individualized task. What I like, or dislike, in a voice might be quite different from what you like or dislike. Neither of us is right or wrong. We each have our own internal models.

Take some time to listen to voices in your home and office, on television, in church, or in the store. Select three or four of the best voices. What is it that you like about them? Easy to listen to? Pitch? Quality? Sincerity? Now select three or four of the poorest voices you have heard. What is it about these voices that turn you off? Are they too loud, brash, grating, nasal, or any of the other negative voice descriptors we listed in Chapter 1?

Now go back and listen to your own voice on a recording. See if you can find the qualities in your own voice that you like in other voices. You can build upon these by following some of the suggestions in this book. If you hear qualities in your voice that you don't like, see if you can eliminate them. Sometimes your ability to compare a good voice model to your own voice is the most important step in helping you improve your voice.

Finding one's natural voice and using it in most talking situations will give most women the voice they want—and deserve.

CHAPTER 14

The Male Voice

*"We told him to step up to the mike,
and speak like a man. It worked."*

Like his female counterpart, the modern American man has learned that his voice conveys a large part of his image to others. Often it is not what he says but how he says it that matters to his listeners. If his voice sends false and negative messages about him, a book like this may be able to help him. A man's natural voice generally sounds best in all circumstances, and is made with the least amount of effort. On those occasions when he needs a different voice, his natural voice is still the foundation voice, the "home base" for whenever he wishes to speak.

In this chapter, we look at the male voice from childhood through old age. We consider the physical factors that distinguish men's voices from women's. We examine the voice problems common to men. And, finally, we offer suggestions to help men use their natural vices to their best advantage.

The Male Voice

As we all know, males speak in a lower pitch than females, except in early childhood (up to age 10) when there is little pitch difference between the sexes. Eleven-year-old girls generally have slightly lower pitched voices than boys the same age because the female generally begins puberty several years earlier.

165

Puberty begins in most boys around the age of 10 and from beginning to end lasts about four years. With an increase of the male hormone testosterone, there is a gradual lowering of voice pitch. These voice changes usually begin in the second year of puberty. By age 14, the male voice pitch has dropped nearly an octave, close to D (147 Hz) below middle C.

During the last six months of puberty, about one-third of all boys experience temporary upward pitch breaks, caused by rapid laryngeal growth. These breaks are normal and disappear entirely as the larynx completes its growth. By age 18, the typical young man has the speaking voice of an adult male, near C (131 Hz) below middle C. His voice pitch will gradually lower over the succeeding years (Figure 14–1). In his early 70s, pitch levels may begin to rise slightly in most males.

During the rapid adolescent voice changes, some boys may exhibit a slight hoarseness, although many do not. For most of their adult years the majority of men have clear voices, except when the voice is affected by things such as allergies, infections, or heavy smoking. However, a rougher voice may again appear after age 70, as shown in Figure 14–1. But recent studies have shown that older men who are physically fit seem free of the hoarseness that less physically fit men experience as they age.

As we noted in the last chapter, the normal male voice tends to inflect downward at the end of sentences and phrases, whereas the female voice tends to inflect upward. The dropping inflection is associated with sureness, and the rising inflection with uncertainty. Panels of listeners asked to evaluate voice recordings generally rate speakers whose inflections fall at the end of sentences as "knowing what they are talking about."

These subjective responses seem to be the result of cultural conditioning, as are the inflection habits themselves. Pitch and voice quality are primarily determined by physical causes. But voice inflections and word stresses seem to be culturally determined, shaped by what the man hears in his everyday life.

Obviously, it makes a great deal of difference in your efforts to control how you speak whether a particular voice characteristic is physically or culturally conditioned. Let us first look at the physical factors that affect the male voice.

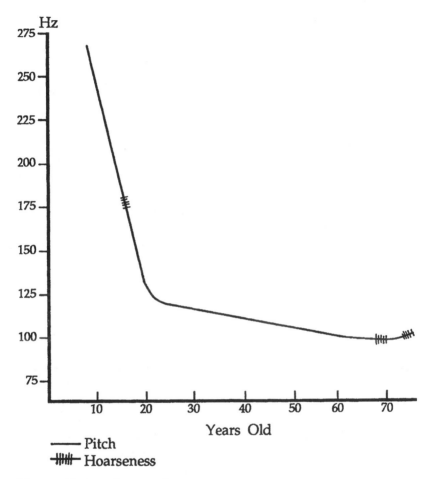

Figure 14–1. Male voice changes over time.

Physical Causes of Male Voice Changes

Around age 10, boys and girls have similar-sized vocal folds, about 10 mm long, and about the same thickness. Boy and girl singers at this age are usually both sopranos. Toward the end of puberty, the male larynx has doubled in size with the vocal folds around 20 mm long. The adult male larynx is also markedly different in composition than the adult female with more and larger striated muscle fiber, less tissue fat, and larger cartilages. It also becomes visually prominent, producing the bulge in the front of the neck that is often called the "Adam's apple." These longer, thicker vocal folds produce a voice that has dropped pitch an octave below prepubertal levels and generally a half an octave lower than a woman's voice.

Male larynges vary greatly in size from man to man. The differences appear to be related primarily to genetic factors, rather than environmental conditions or diet. They also seem unrelated to overall physical stature: tenors, with smaller larynges, come in all heights, sizes, and shapes, as do baritones and basses.

While the majority of men in their 20s, 30s, 40s, and 50s have clear, normal voices, some men develop hoarseness. This can begin in teenage years if they have yelled a lot while playing sports, or were engaged in something like cheerleading. With vocal abuse coming from something like frequent yelling, the vocal fold membranes become thicker and irritated, which may result in a hoarse voice. The thickening and hoarseness often goes away when the habit of yelling stops.

Heavy smoking is another vocal fold irritant. Over time, the smoker's vocal folds become reddened, irritated, and thickened. Under such conditions, it would be hard not to have a hoarse voice. Continuous exposure to other kinds of smoke, fumes, or dust can also produce irritation resulting in hoarseness. And hoarseness is also a common symptom of our bouts with allergies and infections. In these cases, when the source of irritation is eliminated, the voice symptoms usually disappear.

There is a slight, progressive increase in vocal fold thickness among men during their mature years, which lowers their speaking pitch. While at age 20 a man's speaking pitch may be at C (131 Hz) below middle C, by age 50, it has dropped a few notes to an A (110 Hz) or a G (98 Hz).

Around age 70, the hormonal balance between estrogen and testosterone begins to change in men. Consequently, the male begins to lose some vocal fold tissue, which results in a slight elevation of pitch. There can also be some increased hoarseness. An actor who wanted to portray a man in his 90s might be advised to speak in a higher voice and add a bit of hoarseness —a Walter Brennan voice. Speaking a bit slower could also add to the illusion.

The Social Aspects of Men's Voices

Men's and women's voices remain different in contemporary society, despite the occasional androgynous rock star and rising unisex fashions. Nor have changes in the relations between the sexes in the workplace, socially, and in the home produced a tendency for men and women to speak like one another. Indeed, as we saw in the previous section, physical factors would make this difficult even if men or women found it desirable.

Women who have moved into positions that were traditionally held exclusively by men sometimes try to alter the way they speak in certain situations, perhaps to sound more authoritative. But this is more a matter of changing patterns of stress and inflection, not the basic feminine characteristics of their voices.

Although men have not noticeably tried to feminize their voices, even when they work largely with or for women, some men may try to sound even more masculine in such situations. Others make some effort to soften the way they speak around women (many men have long done this socially) from the more aggressive speaking manner they normally use in strictly male company.

Occasionally, there is a man who feels trapped in a male body and desires to become a female. Most such transsexuals (changing from one sex to another gender) are men who are moving toward becoming female. Specific to voice-speech change, the male-to-female transsexual can sound more feminine by prolonging vowels, slightly elevating voice pitch, and inflecting voice upward at the end of sentences. Elevating voice pitch plays only a minor role in the perception of femininity; rather, gestures and employing female mannerisms appear to be more effective in contributing to the female image.

What men have in common with women in an era of changing work roles are voice problems related to using many different voices during the day. Jerry, the owner of a busy restaurant in a California resort city, is a good example. At home in the morning, he liked to wrestle and romp with his two children, and make lots of funny noises to amuse them. With the children off to school, he changed to a softer, caring voice with his wife before he went to work. At work, he used a softer voice greeting customer diners but was often forced to use a louder voice in the kitchen with his cooks and busboys. He always reached the restaurant at the beginning of a hectic lunch hour, and he was instantly in high gear, using a louder, higher pitched voice to be heard over the clatter of glasses and dishes, the buzz of conversation, and the restaurant's background noise. After a relatively quiet voice in the afternoon, he struggled with his voice again through the dinner hour. By the time he arrived home again, his voice was very hoarse.

It was his wife who suggested Jerry come to our voice clinic, after the good night croak began to show up in the daytime, too. "He used to have such a pleasant voice," she said, "almost like a television announcer's. Now he sounds as if he's swallowed a rasp and is mad at me and everyone else."

We were able to help Jerry by first helping him to find his natural voice, which then became the foundation for the different voices he needed in the variety of speaking circumstances he faced every day. Jerry found that his natural voice came out easily with little effort, and was available to him whenever he needed it.

We hear good and bad male voices around us every day. A good voice is usually one that is appropriate for his age and sex and for the circumstances he is experiencing. At the same time, his voice is distinctively his own. His natural voice is easy to produce and does not overtax his vocal equipment.

Public figures often have developed such good voices. Consider a few:

- *Gregory Peck.* Whenever we see an old film of this great actor, we are impressed with his deep resonant voice. It projects an image of sureness.
- *Tom Cruise.* His is a youthful voice, natural, clear, and always at the right pitch level for a person in his mid-40s, regardless of the role he is playing.
- *Barack Obama.* Whatever our political bias may be, we must acknowledge that President Obama always has a clear, strong, and convincing voice.
- *James Earl Jones.* This fine actor has a beautifully resonant voice. Although he has a deep pitch, he keeps absolute

oral focus. His is probably one of the most outstanding voices in this country.

Some men's voices are distinctively different from the way most men talk. In some cases, what is bad about such voices may be responsible for the shaping of the person's public image and success. Because of this, we tend to think of their voices as different rather than bad. The three men listed below have different voices with qualities that could be considered bad.

- *Harry Belafonte.* Although his singing voice is hauntingly beautiful, it is difficult to listen to his higher pitched persistently hoarse speaking voice.
- *Truman Capote.* We enjoyed hearing the effeminate voice of this personality on television, with his many voice pauses followed by many low-to-high upward pitch glides.
- *George Burns.* His hoarse voice had been part of his radio and television image for his whole career. Because of his hoarseness, he often could not speak loudly enough for some people to hear him comfortably.

You can probably add some good and bad male speaking voices to these lists. If you develop an awareness of the qualities that make them good or bad, you can set better goals for your own voice. Keep in mind that it is your natural voice that you are looking for, not a celebrity voice, or a voice that is different just for the sake of sounding different.

Common Problems of the Male Voice

A natural voice is one produced in a way that will not cause voice problems to develop. Unfortunately, men tend to abuse their vocal mechanisms more than women do, and so problems frequently appear. Let us look at some of the problems common to the adult male voice.

Inappropriate Use of Pitch

Some men, and some women, believe that the male image is enhanced by speaking in as low a pitch as possible. But speaking at the bottom of one's pitch range requires a lot of muscle tension. As a result, the voice can sound strained and lack resonance. Moreover, the low-pitched voice often has a low sounding focus, coming from deep down in the throat, which makes it difficult to hear in noisy situations.

Perhaps because the social penalties are too great, relatively few men speak in a high pitch. But some do, and this can also strain the vocal equipment, Finding and using your natural pitch, as shown in Chapter 7, is a good way to overcome problems of a too-low or too-high pitch.

Inappropriate Loudness Levels

Men frequently work in noisier environments than women do. Not only can this create voice strain from trying to speak over the noise all day, but many men also use the same loud voice when they leave the job. Men are usually noisier in their play than women, in their sports, and in some social occasions. One of the ways men seem to assert their masculinity is by talking louder. Listen to a group of teenage boys practicing being macho by using louder voices or to a group of men watching a ball game at a stadium or in a bar.

Men also use a louder voice as a way of controlling people around them, whether at work, play, or in the home. The man who does this frequently is the man who does not adjust his loudness for different situations—loudness may be a hard thing for him to relinquish.

Other men talk too softly, so softly they are hard to understand, and they often project an image of timidity, particularly among other males. Some soft talkers can have a physical problem, perhaps respiratory or neurological, that makes it impossible for them to speak any louder. But usually they talk softly out of long habit, for reasons that have to do with their overall personality. The habitual soft-talker, like the habitual loud-talker, does not adjust his voice volume for the situation.

Loudness adjustment, however, is a key to being heard and understood. The soft-talker might not be heard. The loud-talker might not be understood, or might be resented, and so his message may be ignored. Chapter 6 showed you how to adjust the loudness of your voice so that it is appropriate when you need it.

Yelling

Some men love to yell. Yelling should be avoided because it is so hard on the voice, but that is not always possible. In certain types of industrial plants and on construction sites, men often have to communicate by yelling. And a yelling voice is sometimes necessary in many competitive sports. In all of these situations communication is important, but when they have to yell, many men do so in a low-pitched voice. Many men (if a yell is needed) don't know how to do it. If you need to yell now and then, go back to Chapters 5 (on breath support) and 6 (on loudness). If a loud yell is needed, do it with proper breath support and at the right pitch level.

A star quarterback had a problem yelling at the beginning of his professional career. He had difficulty making his signals heard. When his team was on the road in enclosed arenas such as Seattle's Kingdome, his players couldn't hear the plays he called over the crowd noise. The quarterback felt that several games had been lost because of this. We found that when he tried to bark out his signals, it was in the gruffest, loudest voice he could produce. Once he was taught to yell in a higher pitched voice with good mouth focus, his play-calling could be heard above any but the most raucous crowd noise, and his voice lasted for all four quarters.

To protect the voice, as well as to keep speech understandable, men who must yell should take in bigger breaths, say fewer words on one breath, and use a higher pitch with good oral focus.

Throat Focus

Men are more likely than women to speak with low throat focus, from deep back in their throats. This can produce a voice that is hoarse and hard to hear. Throughout this book we have pointed out that the best sounding voice sounds as if it comes right off the surface of your tongue and in the middle of your mouth.

We have also found that good focus is somewhat independent of pitch. That is, you can have a low-pitched voice and still have high mouth focus. In Chapter 8, and later in this chapter, we tell you some easy ways to develop better oral focus.

Pitch Breaks

Upward pitch breaks are embarrassing to men who have them. We are not talking about pitch breaks experienced by some adolescent boys, which disappear with maturity. We speak of adult men whose voices occasionally break upward. If they gave an order, it might sound like this, with the two marked words breaking up an octave from the regular pitch.

I told you to get off the fence.

Fortunately, such a problem is easy to correct. All the man has to do is raise his regular speaking voice one or two notes and the pitch breaks usually disappear. Upward pitch breaks in men are usually caused by habitually speaking at a pitch level that is too low and is being produced with some strain. The voice escapes this uncomfortable range from time to time by breaking upward. A slight raising of your customary pitch usually gets rid of the problem.

Singing the Wrong Part

Many of us sing from time to time in a church choir, glee club, or community theater musical, as well as in informal gatherings of friends. Singing can be harmful to a man's voice if he sings the wrong part—and this can happen even in more formally organized groups. Choral music frequently is divided into four parts: soprano, alto for women, tenor, and bass for men. Often it does not include a part for baritones, even though that is the normal singing range for most men. The result is that men are often forced to sing higher as tenors or lower as basses.

After an extended stretch of this, the tenor or bass who is really a baritone may feel some throat dryness and pain. He may even find that he has difficulty speaking in his regular voice range and his speaking voice may show some hoarseness. These symptoms disappear as if by magic by not singing the extremes of the singing part, avoiding the highest notes of the tenor range or the lowest notes of the bass range. If you are singing with an organized group, consultation with the choir director, or with a singing teacher, can be helpful. If you are singing more informally, be alert to the symptoms we noted above, and take the necessary steps to ease the problem.

Voice Tips for the Adult Male

As is true for women, men's voices are called on for a variety of roles in work, social, and family life. For men who are salesmen, lawyers, and teachers, voice is vital to their livelihood. In occupations like farmer or author, voice is used far less. But all of us need our voices to represent us well some of the time at work, and it is always important socially or at home to have a voice that represents the real you. Although most men would profit using their natural voice in most situations, there are times when, temporarily, they need to sound a little different. For example, a judge annoyed by the performance of a lawyer in court cannot always afford the luxury of letting that annoyance show in his voice. (Even less can a lawyer let his voice show that he is annoyed with a judge!) But all men face circumstances when they do not want their voices to betray their feelings, or when they need their voices to convey a little more conviction or authority.

Let us look at some things that men can do to better control the way they sound.

Use Pitch and Pitch Changes to Get Your Message Across

You can add authority to your voice by lowering your pitch level. This should be done sparingly. If you always speak at the bottom of your pitch range, it is impossible to inflect your voice any lower when you want to add authority. If you keep it too low, you also run the risk of pitch breaks.

A man comfortable with himself will use rising inflections now and then. Pitch elevation at the end of occasional sentences will encourage your listeners to speak up and ask questions.

Use Loudness and Loudness Changes for Emphasis

There is nothing more boring than listening to someone give (or read) a speech in the same monotonous voice, never varying his loudness. Or the man who always talks in a loud voice who sounds boorish and intimidating. His voice is saying, "I'm talking! Don't interrupt!" or "I'm the only one with all the answers."

On the other hand, a man who always speaks softly is often viewed as timid and unsure of himself. Although he may have a lot to say, what he says may not always be heard. A good guideline is to speak as loudly as the people around you. A soft-spoken person needs to take in slightly larger breaths and say fewer words per breath. Like the habitual talker, he needs to be careful not to sound monotonous and he needs to vary his loudness. Chapter 6 can help men who need better control over the loudness of their voices.

Keep the Right Voice Focus

Pay close attention to well-focused voices like those of such actors as Tom Hanks or Harrison Ford. Regardless of what pitch they use, their voices always sound as if voice focus is in the front of their mouths. They are easy to hear and easy to understand.

The most common voice focus problem for men is a voice that sounds as if it comes from way back and low in the throat. A few men have voices too far forward in focus, sounding the way Truman Capote did with a thin, effeminate voice. A thin-sounding voice usually can be corrected just by bringing the tongue a bit farther back. Men who have the problem of focus too far back in the throat can correct it by bringing the tongue a little forward when they speak. A little practice with tongue positions, using your audio or video recorder, will help you make the voice focus differences.

Further suggestions for developing good voice focus can be found in Chapter 8. The benefits of a well-focused voice are that it can always be heard, sounds better, and does not tire easily.

Change the Friendliness in Your Voice

There are times when we don't want to sound friendly, when an unfriendly voice may be necessary or useful. We may find ourselves in a relatively rare situation where a friendly voice is simply inappropriate. A frown and a down-turned mouth, the opposite of a smile, will color the sound of your voice. You can also show displeasure by lowering your pitch level and dropping your word inflections at the end of phrases and sentences with some finality.

Most of the time most of us want to sound friendly. Both at work and in our social lives we get more positive results when we do. The problem is that some men normally have unfriendly voices, particularly on the telephone. Without wanting to, or even being aware of it, they may sound angry or irritated most of the time.

There are several things one can do to have a more friendly sounding voice, For one thing, smile more as you talk. Research studies show that people listening to recorded voices can tell whether or not the speaker was smiling. The act of smiling influences the sound of the voice—try it with your recorder and you should hear the difference. Laughter does the same thing. It seems to open up the throat, lessen the tension of oral and facial muscles and relax the voice, making the speaker sound more friendly and less negative. We often encourage laughter for our patients who have severe tense voices.

You will also sound friendlier when you feel happy inside. Take a moment before speaking to ask someone to reflect on your mood. Let happiness show in your voice. You'll speak faster and often with some humor.

Listen to your regular voice on a recorder. Do you sound like a friendly person? If you do, fine—remember that sound.

If you don't, but you want to, try some of these suggestions we just suggested (smile and laugh more).

Some Voice Tips to Include Others in the Conversation

Many men talk too much. Competitive as we are, we try to dominate the conversation in groups and don't always take the time to let others talk, or to listen to them when they do.

Healthy, normal conversation is a two-way affair: we talk-we listen, we talk-we listen. By using low pitch, loudness, and falling inflections, many men control conversation instead. It may do something for their egos, or anxieties, but it is not true conversation, and it often stirs up resentment and resistance among listeners.

A lot of men control conversations this way just out of habit. They have become insensitive to the fact that each conversational situation requires a different approach. Or they simply don't know how to help create a conversation in which all parties participate.

An obvious way to get listener participation is by directly asking questions of others. Or rising vocal inflections at the ends of phrases and sentences also invite listeners to respond with their ideas. If we couple this with a smiling face, the invitation is even clearer (and it is friendly).

You can experiment with these techniques using your recorder. Try reading or improvising some sentences that you might normally use in your work, but give rising inflections to the ends of phrases or sentences, where you want to encourage listener participation. Don't forget to pause a bit, so they have time to speak up. And don't overdo it, so you sound as if you're unsure of yourself. That is where a smile can really help. A slight rising inflection along with a smile clearly signals that you want to hear from your listeners. If you have video on your smartphone, listen and watch yourself on playback.

Men, as well as women, will find that using their natural voices in the various roles they are called on to play will give them the best sounding voice, and the most effective one. In situations when circumstances require them to play a particular part, a different voice may be required temporarily. There are techniques for doing that, too, as we have shown.

By this point in the book, you have found your natural voice, your natural breathing, loudness, pitch, and focus, and you have learned something about using it even in special or difficult circumstances. It is time now to give you a summary of the techniques needed to maintain your natural voice so that it is always there for you to use when you want it.

CHAPTER 15

Ten Steps for Keeping Your Natural Voice

"A good maintenance program for your natural voice is neither difficult nor time consuming."

Most of us are aware today that taking care of our health involves more than going to see a doctor when we don't feel well. Millions now follow some regular exercise programs and are careful about how much and what foods we eat. We have learned that there is a great deal we can do ourselves to keep us healthy.

A healthy, natural voice benefits from the same kind of awareness and attention. Now that you have corrected some of the problems you might have had with your voice, and have learned to use your natural voice, you can easily keep it that way by following the maintenance program in this chapter. It is neither difficult nor time consuming. All you need to do is use this chapter from time to time as a reminder and review.

Use your audio or video recorder, which was so helpful in many of the previous tests and exercises, to record a few minutes of both conversation and reading. Then listen and/or watch critically to the playback.

We have gone through this book and developed a summary of voice behaviors and grouped them into a single table (Table 15–1). This nominal list can help you find whether each dimension of your voice is where you want it to be. Listen to your recording and rate yourself on each dimension. A normal or natural rating on the Voice Checklist is a 4. Extreme problems

Table 15–1. The Voice Checklist

Voice Dimension	Ratings						
Breathing (words per breath)	1	2	3	4	5	6	7
	Too Few			Normal			Too Many
Loudness	1	2	3	4	5	6	7
	Soft			Natural			Too Loud
Pitch	1	2	3	4	5	6	7
	Low			Natural			High
Pitch Inflections	1	2	3	4	5	6	7
	None			Normal			Excessive
Horizontal Focus	1	2	3	4	5	6	7
	Back			Normal			Front
Vertical Focus	1	2	3	4	5	6	7
	Throat			Normal			Nasal
Nasality	1	2	3	4	5	6	7
	Denasal			Balanced			Hypernasal
Quality	1	2	3	4	5	6	7
	Breathy			Normal Quality			Harsh Tight

of voice on the scale would be a 1 or 7. Most of the time, if we still find we have a problem with voice, the problem is slight (a 3 or 5 on the scale) or is moderate (a 2 or 6 rating).

Any of the voice problems mentioned in this book can range from slight to severe. Throughout the book, for purposes of illustration, we have usually presented severe cases. In reality, most of our voice problems are more likely to be slight or moderate problems with breathing, loudness, pitch, focus, or nasality. If you have rated yourself different than normal on any items of the Voice Checklist, you will probably want to go back and review the chapter dealing with that particular problem; then, do the exercises suggested until you feel the problem has been reduced.

Whether your voice problem is only slight or occasional, it still may be a problem that may need attention. First of all, you want always to sound your best. Second, some slight voice problems have a way of developing into severe ones, and some occasional problems can turn into permanent ones. Third, even if that is not the case, a slight problem can draw a negative reaction from your listeners. A voice with slight nasality or denasality can be hard on your listeners; similarly, a voice that is always slightly too loud or too soft, too high or low in pitch can be a negative for your listeners.

If you have given yourself 4s, or normal scores, on all of the items, good for you. That is what we designed this book to do, to enable you to find and use your natural voice consistently, to present yourself through your voice as the person you really are. If you have no voice problem, you can greatly benefit from a regular program of natural voice maintenance, from staying aware of those things that are most helpful or most harmful for good voice.

Just as you may keep a list of healthy and unhealthy food ingredients, or a reminder on your closet door of exercises you want to perform each day, you may want to keep a list of the ten steps to remember for keeping a healthy natural voice.

Ten Easy Steps for Keeping Your Natural Voice

1. Cut Down on Throat Clearing and Coughing, Avoid Yelling

Many potentially good voices are destroyed by vocal abuse. Three of the most common abuses are throat clearing, excessive coughing, and yelling. Throat clearing is hard on the voice, and is often more of a habit than a necessity. When you clear your throat, you may raise a small amount of mucus but the act itself bangs the vocal folds together unnecessarily and can cause some tissue irritation. The irritated mucosal tissue then produces its own protective mucus. The process becomes self-generating: the more you clear your throat, the more you need to do so.

Habitual throat clearers need to make a conscious effort to curb the habit. One way to do it is to sniff with intensity as a substitute for clearing the throat. This quick sniff can rid the vocal folds of some mucus, and we then swallow what we sniff.

Another way to clear your throat is to do it as silently as you can. Silent throat clearing is much less irritating to the vocal folds.

Continuous heavy coughing is also hard on the vocal folds. High-speed photography of the larynx during a cough shows that the vocal folds slam together and are blown apart suddenly by the outgoing air. As a result of this trauma, continued heavy coughing can result in swollen, irritated vocal folds, which make normal voice almost impossible.

Often there is a physical cause for continuous coughing, such as a bad cold, an allergy, or smoky air. Such conditions may require medical treatment. Some coughing, however, has become a habit, just as throat clearing does. For this kind of habit we need to practice the "silent cough," as silently as we can. Cough as quietly as you can. The silent cough is far easier on the vocal folds than the loud cough that most of us usually make.

Yelling is very hard on the voice, and we need to avoid yelling whenever possible. Except in rare emergencies, most yelling is not necessary. If you must yell on occasion, do it sensibly. Use a lot of breath behind your voice, a higher pitch, and good mouth focus. This will enable your voice to carry with better volume. Still, if you want to keep a better voice, the less you yell the better.

2. Develop an Easy Vocal Attack (Use Southern Speech)

Hard voice attack is related to the degree of abruptness with which we say our words. In music, the opposite of hard attack is called legato, where there are no discernible breaks between notes. In voice, an easy attack blends words and sounds together gently, as in a Southern accent. We hear that easy voicing in the voice of Jimmy Carter. Listen to his easy speech. A hard, abrupt attack can be heard in many Northeastern voices, such as those of Don Adams or Bette Davis.

The soft, legato-like voice is a lot easier on the vocal folds and on the ears of our listeners. Hard voice attack takes too much effort. The larynx tires easily and the vocal folds can become irritated from such continuous abrupt usage. Between talking abruptly or with an easy voice attack, there is no contest. The easy voice sounds better and it doesn't strain or tire the larynx.

3. Use a Pitch Level That Is Natural for You

Many men try to sound authoritative by speaking at the bottom of their pitch ranges. Some professional women also attempt to sound more in command by speaking with too low a pitch. Other people use voices that are pitched too high. As we pointed out in Chapter 7, most of us will get better mileage out of our voices by using an average pitch level that is only several notes above our lowest note.

When we talk about your best pitch level, we are speaking of the level that is easy and natural for you, the level you will probably use about 70% of the time when you speak. But none of us should have an absolute pitch level that we use all the time. Varying our pitch up and down as we stress particular words or syllables gives our voice needed inflections. It makes our speech livelier, more interesting, and avoids the dull monotone.

In Chapter 7, you found your natural pitch level. That is the baseline for your pitch, and it is the level at which you will usually sound your best.

4. Develop Good Horizontal and Vertical Voice Focus

Many people have voices that sound as if they come from deep in their throats. Other voices are focused too high in the nose and sound nasal. Still others are produced too far forward (the baby voice) or too far back (the Alf voice). A good, natural voice sound comes from the imagery of being focused right on the top of your tongue in the middle of your mouth. It is also an efficient voice and one that can stand up to a lot of use. A voice with good focus is durable and will always be there when you need it.

5. Renew Your Breath More Often by Pausing

Renewing your breath more often as you speak is important for keeping your natural voice and avoiding vocal strain. Trying to speak without adequate air, by muscular exertion alone, is a real workout for the vocal tract.

There are two ways to develop good breathing habits while speaking. First, become aware of how many words you can easily say on one breath. If you run out of air as you speak, try to use a fraction (say one-half) of the number of words you say before you pause again to renew your breath.

Second, learn when to pause. There are natural breaks in what we say that easily permit a pause: before an important word (the pause preceding it gives it more emphasis), or wherever there is a comma or period in a written text, or at the ends of phrases and sentences. The pause provides you with an automatic renewal of breath. With a good breath supply behind your vibrating vocal folds, you should easily be able to maintain a good, natural voice.

6. Reduce Your Demands on Your Voice. Don't Do All the Talking

Some voices are destroyed by overwork. To maintain a healthy, natural voice it is important to avoid excessive talking. It has been my observation over the years that many of the people with voice problems have such gregarious personalities that they talk all the time. Friendly chattiness, and being the life of the party, is fine. But overdoing it can result in negative voice symptoms such as hoarseness or a voice that becomes weak or faint at the end of the day.

If symptoms do appear, a conscious effort to cut down talking, or simply being quiet, will often help to renew a tired voice. Many people, like teachers, have to use their voices a lot because of the kind of work they do. They cannot cut down the amount of talking they do. For them, the nine other suggestions in this chapter can be of great help in maintaining the best possible voice under demanding conditions. A voice that is used a lot needs to be used properly.

7. Develop a Relaxed Vocal Tract. Remember the Yawn-Sigh

Many voices are impaired by tightening of the vocal tract, by shutting down the larynx, the throat, and the mouth. A voice produced like that sounds tense and often lacks volume and normal resonance. There are several things that we can do to develop a more open, relaxed vocal tract.

Keep your mouth open more. A slight opening between your lips, and a gentle opening (not much wider than the thickness of a pocket comb) between your upper and lower front teeth (your incisors) can contribute a great deal to developing an easy, relaxed voice. An open vocal tract can be developed even when you are not talking. While you listen to someone else, or when you read or watch television, make a deliberate effort to keep your mouth slightly open.

Remember the yawn-sigh. No other vocal technique opens up a tight vocal tract as quickly as this one. The vocal tract opens maximally when we yawn. The yawn inhalation creates an open airway, and the exhaled sigh that follows produces a relaxed voice, primarily because the vocal resonating tract is still open. In situations where your throat feels tense and your voice sounds tight, feel the oral relaxation that the yawn-sigh can give you.

8. Avoid Talking in Loud Settings. Watch the Noise Level

Talking against a background of loud noise can strain anyone's voice. One of the noisiest backgrounds around would be a live rock concert in an arena or auditorium. In such loud noise exposure, people cannot monitor their own voices, and they end up shouting and adding to the general din. Many bars and restaurants have not only a loud television set going but background music as well. After prolonged attempts to talk in such a loud setting, one often experiences symptoms of vocal fatigue, throat discomfort, and possible hoarseness.

Other settings where background noise can be a problem are less obvious. Conversing during a long car ride or on a commercial jet, or at a ball game can tire your voice. Talking above loud music at home, speaking next to power mowers or leaf blowers, or talking at home against the noise of a vacuum clearer or a microwave can be taxing on the voice. To preserve your voice in such loud settings, attempt to reduce the amount of talking that you do.

If you must talk in such noisy places, your voice will last longer if you speak with a vertical focus and a slightly higher pitch level. And remember, the louder you speak the more air you need. At these louder levels, you should say fewer words between breaths.

9. Avoid Smoking and Excessive Use of Alcohol

The person who needs to use his or her voice a lot, and wants to maintain a natural voice, should avoid smoking. The mucous membranes of the throat and vocal folds become inflamed and swollen from the dryness, heat, and tars from tobacco smoke. If you experience persistent hoarseness or other vocal problems as a result of smoking, a trial period of not smoking may be all that is needed to restore the voice to normal. Incidentally, marijuana is a much hotter smoke than smoke from regular tobacco cigarettes and, therefore, a greater vocal fold irritant.

Mild (two drinks a day or less) or occasional use of alcohol seems to have no negative effects on the voice. Heavier daily use (three or more drinks) can often have negative effects. Excessive alcohol may dilate the tiny blood vessels in the membranes covering the vocal folds, resulting in a lower pitch with some hoarseness—the voice of the well-known "whiskey tenor."

10. Watch Your Water Needs: Humidity and Liquids

Excessive dryness is hard on the voice. I often tell my clients that "a healthy voice is a wet one." People who are concerned about their voices should pay attention to both the amount of liquid they drink and the dryness of the air they breathe. Excessive dryness can irritate the membranes covering the vocal folds and cause swelling. On examination of patients with excessively dry mouths, we also find some redness and red-streaking of the membranes in the back of the throat. Such irritation often is eliminated completely by drinking more fluids.

Certain medications can also have drying effects on the vocal tract. Antihistamines have an immediate drying effect. There are, however, antihistamines available that contain a moisturizer, an important help for those who must use their voice a lot but who have to take antihistamines. Drugs, such as diuretics, often used for the treatment of high blood pressure, can also cause extensive dryness of the throat and larynx. People who take such medications should check with their doctors or pharmacists to see if the drug has a side effect of throat dryness. If dryness is a problem, there are some saliva-producing medications that can be used.

The humidity of the air we breathe can affect how we sound. One reason that singers favor nose-breathing inhalation is that air passing through the nose and throat becomes warmer and more moist. Some moisture in the air is essential for normal voice. Humidity under 20%, or over 70%, may require you to do something to change the moisture level in your environment. Air conditioners and gas furnaces can remove much of the humidity from the air. You may need a humidifier or vaporizer to add more moisture. In damp climates, air conditioners and dehumidifiers may be required to remove excess moisture from the air.

In follow-up studies of patients with voice problems, we have found that changing the humidity levels (higher or lower) in rooms where they live, sleep, or work can have positive effects in decreasing their negative voice symptoms.

This chapter is probably all that most of you will need in the future to maintain the good, natural voice that you have found with the help of this book. Re-reading parts of the book from time to time may refresh your memory about the good voice habits you have learned, and about the bad habits you need to avoid.

The following chapter is intended primarily for those of you who have not been able to eliminate your voice problems.

It can also be of help for any user of voice who wants to know what professional help is available for difficult or persistent voice problems.

CHAPTER 16

Professional Help for Voice Problems

"Some of my friends could use help with their voices."

After reading the previous chapters, you probably have developed a new awareness of your own voice and the voices around you. You have a more accurate idea of how you sound. You know what voice practices can give you a bad voice and what things you can do to develop a better, more natural voice. You probably also remember that a sudden change of voice, such as hoarseness that lasts for more than seven days, despite what you do to improve it, should be investigated by a physician.

This seven-day rule for sudden and continued hoarseness is a good one to remember. Although this book is about adult voice problems and voice improvement, the seven-day rule is particularly important to keep in mind for children, 16 years old and younger. Hoarseness in children can be a symptom of serious laryngeal disease. Few children between the ages of 2 and 13 develop hoarse voices without some underlying physical cause. It is rare for them to become hoarse or to lose their voices completely for purely functional reasons. If your own child has persistent hoarseness, take him or her to a doctor or ear-nose-throat specialist (otolaryngologist).

Other voice symptoms that may require the help of other specialists include pain associated with heavy voice use, or complete loss of voice, or inability to speak louder, or continued nasality. Pain while speaking, particularly after long, continued speaking, is not normal and should be investigated medically. A complete loss of voice (aphonia) from some physical cause might be best treated, also, by an otolaryngologist. Loss of voice that persists without physical cause might be best treated by the speech-language pathologist, perhaps in collaboration with a psychologist or psychiatrist. Lack of voice loudness can usually be improved by many of the specialists who work with people with voice disorders. A nasal voice might first be evaluated by the speech-language pathologist who could then decide what other specialists might be needed.

In short, not all adult voice problems can be helped by reading and practicing with a book like this. It can be a helpful supplement when you are working with other materials or treatments prescribed by one of the specialists listed below. If you need more help than we have been able to give you, or if your voice problem is still there despite your efforts with our brief exercises, you need to consult an expert in the particular problem area of voice that concerns you. For your convenience, we have listed the specialists who work with voice problems in alphabetical order with a brief description of what each person does. This is then followed with a description of how that specialty can help with particular voice problems.

- Allergist: Helps control symptoms of allergy that affect voice.
- Audiologist: Helps when voice problems are related to hearing loss.
- Choir director: Helps develop better breath control for voice.
- Drama teacher: Helps with voice improvement and voice control.
- Endocrinologist: Can help with glandular and hormonal influences on voice.
- Inhalation therapist: Helpful if you have a breathing problem.
- Otolaryngologist: Treats diseases of the ear, nose, and throat.

- Pharmacist: Can advise on side-effects of medications on voice.
- Physiatrist: Prescribes exercises for breath and posture improvement.
- Plastic surgeon: Can treat voice resonance by surgical change of structures.
- Prosthodontist: Can treat voice nasality with dental appliances.
- Psychiatrist: Can help voice problems caused by anxiety and stage fright.
- Psychologist: Can help voice problems related to poor self-image.
- Speech-language pathologist: Provides voice evaluation and therapy for voice problems.
- Speech therapist: Another name for speech-language pathologist.
- Voice coach: Can often improve the singing and/or speaking voice.
- Voice pathologist: Another name for speech-language pathologist.
- Voice scientist: An expert in the mechanisms of normal voice.

Now let us look more thoroughly at each of the specialists with whom we might consult.

Allergist

An allergist is a medical doctor with a board certified specialty in allergies who diagnoses and treats various allergies. Many ear-nose-throat doctors (see otolaryngologist) also have a special interest in allergies related to voice. For problems of phonation and resonance that only seem to present themselves during particular parts of the year, the allergist can often identify particular allergies and provide treatment relief that can be most helpful in reducing voice symptoms.

Audiologist

The audiologist is in a related professional to the speech-language pathologist and should be certified as a clinical audiologist by the American Speech-Language-Hearing Association (ASHA). The audiologist tests hearing and provides habilitative services, such as fitting hearing aids for people with hearing problems. Some problems of hoarseness and faulty resonance can be the direct result of hearing loss. Anyone who suspects that he or she may have a hearing loss should consult an audiologist or an otolaryngologist.

Choir Director

A choir director may be of special help if you have problems coordinating your breathing with your speaking voice. Obviously, if you have a singing problem the choir director can be helpful. But many choir directors know more about breath control and talking than many of the other specialists listed here. Because choir directors have varied backgrounds, you might ask around in your community for the names of the better choir directors.

Drama Teacher

Sometimes the local high school or college drama teacher can be of great help for the person who wants some voice help. An experienced drama coach or teacher can help develop better breathing technique for a better voice. Drama teachers often use mental imagery, encouraging their pupils to develop particular mental states as a preparation for developing a particular voice. Some theater voice techniques can markedly improve your speaking voice for talking in front of groups. However, the drama teacher's voice techniques may be less effective for use in everyday conversation.

Endocrinologist

An endocrinologist is a physician with board certification in endocrinology, the study of the internal secretions and endocrine glands of the body, such as the thyroid or pituitary glands. Occasionally, voice problems are related to problems of glandular or hormonal imbalance, and these are often successfully treated by the endocrinologist.

Inhalation Therapist

The growing number of people with respiratory problems (often related to a history of excessive smoking) has resulted in the emergence of the medically related specialty of inhalation therapy. For the occasional voice patient with a breathing problem, such as emphysema, the inhalation therapist can often be of greater help than any other specialist. An inhalation therapist is usually recommended by the family physician.

Otolaryngologist

The otolaryngologist (sometimes called an otorhinolaryngologist) is a physician with advanced training in the diagnosis and treatment of ear, nose, and throat (ENT) diseases and disorders. The patient who has continued hoarseness for more than seven days should consult an ENT doctor for a throat examination. Speech-language pathologists and audiologists work closely with otolaryngologists. If the voice problem is related to disease of the vocal mechanisms, the ENT doctor would provide the primary treatment. If faulty voice usage appears to be the primary problem, the otolaryngologist will usually refer the patient to a speech-language pathologist for therapy.

Pharmacist

Many people do not realize that pharmacists have more knowledge about drugs and their side effects than any other specialty. If a physician prescribes a medication for a particular medical problem, that drug could also cause some shortness of breath, excessive drying of mouth, or some other symptom that can directly affect voice. Consult your local pharmacist about the medications you take. Taking more than one drug at a time can sometimes cause drug interaction effects. Ask if there are possible side effects that might affect your voice. Sometimes changing from one medication to another can greatly influence the way you sound.

Physiatrist

The physiatrist is a medical doctor who has completed a residency in rehabilitative medicine. He or she often heads a hospital department that may have different names such as Physical Medicine, Rehabilitation, Adaptive Medicine, or Restorative Medicine. Some voice problems are related to accidents and falls from perhaps injuries to the back, neck, or head. Medical problems related to stroke or other neurological disorders may alter one's speech and voice, often requiring referral to the speech-language pathologist. The physiatrist can prescribe exercise programs that will improve breathing control and body posture, which may result in producing a better voice.

Plastic Surgeon

The plastic surgeon is concerned with the repair and restoration of absent, injured, or deformed parts of the body. When someone has a nasality problem related to a deformed palate or throat, the plastic surgeon often can correct the defect so that the nasality will diminish. Usually, even after surgical correction of the palate, voice therapy with a speech-language pathologist is required to develop normal vocal resonance.

Prosthodontist

The prosthodontist is a dentist who specializes in the construction and fitting of dentures, retainers, and palatal lifts (a device that lifts up paralyzed palates). For the occasional person with some kind of neurological problem, such as stroke, the prosthodontist can create an appliance that may help produce better nasal resonance. The person with a cleft palate can often profit from the same kind of appliance, which can prevent the escape of air and voice through the nose and divert it out through the mouth. For the person who has a problem with false teeth affecting speech and voice, the prosthodontist is perhaps the dental specialist best able to correct it.

Psychiatrist

The psychiatrist is a medical doctor with a specialty interest in mental and psychological disorders. For problems of anxiety, depression, or stage fright the psychiatrist uses behavioral techniques (interview, therapy) and organic techniques (drugs) to help patients cope with their problems. When people feel better about themselves and feel happier, their improved mood state is usually heard in their voices. For people with voice problems that appear related to difficulty relating to other people they may profit from seeing a psychiatrist.

Psychologist

Most certified and licensed psychologists have a doctoral degree. The psychologist tests and treats patients with psychological problems such as anxiety, nervousness, and phobias. Psychologists usually offer both group and individual therapy, using various counseling and therapy techniques. People who have voice problems related to anxiety and stress in particular situations may find the psychologist's services invaluable. For many functional

voice problems, the psychologist and speech-language pathologist working together often demonstrate success in helping the
patient find and use a better voice.

Speech-Language Pathologist

These specialists, officially called speech-language pathologists
by their certifying body, the American Speech-Language-Hearing Association (ASHA), have advanced graduate training in the
diagnosis and treatment of various communication disorders.
The names of speech pathologist and speech-language pathologist are often used interchangeably. Of even more confusion to
the outsider, the term SLP is commonly used for designation
of the speech-language pathologist by other members of the
rehab team. Among the professional community of SLPs, there
are many who specialize in the diagnosis and treatment of voice
disorders. The SLP has good success in treating the individual
with problems of hoarseness, nasality, poor voice loudness and
quality, and voice problems related to anxiety or stage fright.

Speech Therapist

The speech therapist is the same professional as a speech-
language pathologist (SLP). The term therapist is no longer used
by ASHA.

Voice Coach

The voice coach is primarily interested in the professional user
of voice, such as the actor, lecturer, or singer. The experience
and training of voice coaches varies. Some are former performers themselves who now specialize in working with clients in
the same area of their performance. Others may have specialized
training in voice, and/or advanced degrees, and work with anyone who feels the need for voice improvement. The voice coach

is often successful in increasing the loudness and improving the quality of problem voices.

Voice Pathologist

Although there is no one specialty called "voice pathologist," some otolaryngologists and some speech-language pathologists who specialize in voice disorders sometimes designate themselves as voice pathologists.

Voice Scientist

A voice scientist is usually a doctoral-level person trained in studying the various aspects of normal voice: respiration, phonation (voicing), and resonance. Although the primary interest of voice scientists is research, some are also clinically certified as either otolaryngologists or speech-language pathologists.

Rather than looking for a voice specialist in the yellow pages of a telephone directory or calling someone on a random hunch, ask around in your community to find specialists knowledgeable about voice disorders. A local medical school or university program in speech-language pathology could direct you to the best specialist for your voice problem. Other good sources of information are your doctor or the speech-language pathologists in a local hospital or in the schools. If you live in a small town, you might have to travel to a larger city to see a voice specialist who knows something about your problem. In the city, be sure to consult with someone who has demonstrated experience with people with voice problems.

Finally, a good source of information for voice problems and their treatment is your state speech-language-hearing organization or the national organizations listed below. When you contact them, describe your voice problem and request the names of clinics and voice specialists in your town or city. You may find Google useful in finding more specific contact information.

Addresses for State and National Organizations

An example for contacting a state organization where you live:

Alaska Speech-Language-Hearing Association (AKSHA)
P.O. Box 111993
Anchorage, AK 99511

National Voice Associations or Organizations:

American Academy of Otolaryngology-Head & Neck
    Surgery (AAO-HNS)
1650 Diagonal Road
Alexandria, VA 22314

American Speech-Language-Hearing Association (ASHA)
2200 Research Blvd.
Rockville, MD 20850

National Association of Teachers of Singing (NATS)
9957 Moorings Drive
Jacksonville, FL 32257

The Voice Foundation
219 North Broad St.
Philadelphia, PA 19107

Voice and Speech Trainers Association (VASTA)
2937 West Liberty Ave.
Pittsburgh, PA 15216

Suggested References

Listed below are a few selected references you might like to review.

Abitbol, J., Abitbol, P., & Abitbol, B. (1999). Sex hormones and the female voice. *Journal of Voice, 13*, 424–446.

Boone, D. R., McFarlane, S. C., Von Berg, S. L., & Zraick, R. I. (2014). *The Voice and Voice Therapy* (9th ed.). Boston, MA: Pearson Education.

Izdebski, K. (2008). *Emotions in the human voice: Culture and perception* (Vol. III). San Diego, CA: Plural.

Linklater, K. (2006). *Freeing the natural voice*. Hollywood, CA: Drama Publishers.

Rosen, C. A., Lee, A. S., Zullo, T., & Murry, T. (2004). Development and validation of the Voice Handicap Index–10. *Laryngoscope, 114*, 1549–1556.

Sauter, D. A., Eisner, F., Calder, A. J., & Scott, S. K. (2010). Perceptual cues in nonverbal vocal expressions of emotions. *Quarterly Journal of Experimental Psychology, 63*, 2251–2272.

Index

Note: Page numbers in **bold** reference non-text material.